Virgin Islands

Berlitz®
Virgin Islands

Text by Lindsay Bennett
Edited by Richard Wallis
Updated by Simon Lee
Photography: All photos by Pete Bennett
(except for page 80)
Cover photograph by Pete Bennett
Photo Editor: Naomi Zinn
Layout: Media Content Marketing, Inc.
Cartography by Ortelius Design
Managing Editor: Tony Halliday

Seventh Edition 2003

CONTACTING THE EDITORS
Every effort has been made to provide accurate information in this publication, but changes are inevitable. The publisher cannot be responsible for any resulting loss, inconvenience or injury. We would appreciate it if readers would call our attention to any errors or outdated information by contacting Berlitz Publishing, PO Box 7910, London SE1 1WE, England. Fax: (44) 20 7403 0290;
e-mail: berlitz@apaguide.demon.co.uk

010/307 RP

CONTENTS

• A (☛) in the text denotes a highly recommended sight

Virgin Islands

THE ISLANDS AND THEIR PEOPLE

Sitting like uncut emeralds in waters that mark the transition between the Atlantic Ocean and the Caribbean Sea, the Virgin Islands are the products of ancient volcanic action. The hills and vales are swathed in vegetation—lush and green with mahogany and ferns, or dry and desert-like with cacti. Around each island a ring of sandy beaches has developed, some with sand fine as talcum and so white that it shines in the sunlight.

The climate of the Virgin Islands is nearly perfect. The sun shines every day, the temperature varies very little, and the constant sea breezes cool the sun's rays, bringing a reassuring rustle to the leaves of palms and sea grapes on the coastal fringes. Rain often arrives at night, bringing much-needed water without spoiling the tropical days.

Over 100 islands make up the chain. There are so many, in fact, that when Columbus caught sight of them in 1493 he named them after the 11,000 virgin followers of St. Ursula, an early Christian martyr. He soon moved on, and this natural beauty and rich natural environment might have remained a secret. But the Virgin Islands' proximity to the treasure of the Spanish Main in the 16th century increased their fame. Spanish galleons sailed back from South America past these islands, and pirate forces used the inlets and coves to lie in wait for the booty. Caches of gold and gems hidden by these cut-throats are said to lie yet undiscovered on the distant beaches of the most remote islands.

> **The Virgin Islands are 1,100 miles (1,760 km) from Miami, 1,600 miles (2,560 km) from New York, and over 3,000 miles (4,800 km) from London.**

Striking gold: Biras Creek, on the North Sound of Virgin Gorda, tinted by the setting sun.

European colonial powers later divided up the tiny region, which eventually became known as the British Virgin Islands and the Danish West Indian Islands. Although the boundaries between the two were entirely man-made, the two societies reflected fascinating cultural and economic differences, many of which are still evident today.

The Danish crown sold its islands (the main ones being St. Croix, St. Thomas, and St. John) to the United States in 1917, and the Danish West Indian Islands became the United States Virgin Islands. Since then America has embraced its little bit of paradise, maintaining the tax-free status bestowed by the Danes and developing a home-away-from-home in the tropics. Officially the islands have "unincorporated territory" status, with a considerable amount of home rule through an elected legislature. There are still many vestiges of Danish rule and island history, particularly on St. Croix, and these are protected with a reverence by national bodies and local people alike.

However, the US Virgin Islands are definitely American, particularly St. Thomas, which as the busiest island welcomes the majority of visitors. Life moves at a relatively fast pace for a small island—cellular phones are essential equipment, as are cars. Fast food doesn't come any faster in Miami or New York. Hotels offer every comfort, and the shopping can't be beat.

St. John is a wonder of nature protected by a forward-thinking and extremely rich benefactor who, in 1956, thought to buy large sections of the island and give it in trust to the government of the US. It is now a natural paradise, a reminder of how the other islands might have looked before development changed their landscape forever. The largest American island, St. Croix, is a pleasing blend of the commercial and the scenic and, perhaps, the most "Caribbean."

> **Slow down to island time. Nothing ever gets rushed here, particularly on the British islands.**

The British Virgin Islands, on the other hand, have remained British since the late 17th century. Following the abolition of slavery in the 1830s, many freed slaves received property from the colonial landowners. They settled down to work their land in what became a settled corner of the Victorian Empire. Today the islands are a British colony, with a governor appointed by the crown. A constitution grants a great deal of self-government from the capital, Road Town, which is on the island of Tortola.

On the British islands, it is easy to forget the rest of the world exists. When crossing the invisible line from the US Virgin Islands to the British, you seem to travel back a few

decades. Cars are a little older, goats and chickens wander freely along the main roads, and tiny painted wooden shacks can be seen nestling in the hillsides. Ties with other British Caribbean islands are still strong, and whether it be rum imported from Barbados or Jamaica or discussions about the progress of the West Indian cricket team, there's a feeling of camaraderie among people who live (or have lived) under the Union Jack.

Water babies: local kids make a splash at Magen's Bay, St. Thomas.

There are a few surprises in store for visitors from both sides of the Atlantic. The US dollar is the official currency used throughout the islands, which might come as a shock to travelers from Britain. You'll even find Royal Mail postage stamps in the British Virgin Islands—the only ones in the world to be priced in American dollars. For Americans, the shock comes when driving. Islanders drive on the left side of the road, a habit left over from the days of Danish rule—although, oddly enough, no one in Denmark ever drove on the left.

Throughout the islands, the common heritage is celebrated in language and music. The Caribbean English dialect is a shared legacy of those born and raised as Virgin Islanders and has developed its own particular vocabulary. On both sides of the border you'll hear the same rhythms and beats encapsulated in the dulcet tones of steel and "scratch" bands, for music is a constant companion to daily life. This is particularly true at carnival time, when the whole community comes together in one massive street party.

Residents, whatever their ancestry, are proud of their roots. They honor their rich and varied history and their essentially harmonious society. Religious faith is still as strong here as it was 100 years ago, as the large number of churches testifies. Most islanders give thanks for the day and for the food they put on the table.

This is a society that today must work hard to avoid becoming a victim of its own economic successes. The Virgin Islands are considered by travelers to be among the world's most beautiful holiday destinations, and rightly so. Some fear that the delicate balance of island life and nature could be upset by the tourist trade and by the increasing numbers of immigrants (from the Caribbean and the US) who come to seek work and an island home.

For visitors, the lure of the Virgin Islands is as much

You can never have too many…T-shirts for sale at a beach market stall.

Keeping a low profile: a simple, whitewashed church strikes an unassuming pose in Great Harbour, Jost Van Dyke.

about the waters that surround them as about the beauties of the land. Tortola, the main British island, is the sailboat charter capital of the world. Every week hundreds of sails unfurl and yachts set out across the channels to anchor in one of a thousand small coves or settle in for the night at a safe harbor.

Underwater life is just as exciting. The water here is among the clearest and most beautiful in the world. In summer the shallows are glassy still and range from azure blue to emerald green, while the ocean channels reflect a deep blue that can most easily be seen from the air. The sandy shallows provide ideal swimming and snorkeling environments. Since the development in the 1930s of SCUBA (Self-Contained Underwater Breathing Apparatus), the seas have provided a whole new world for adventurers. Divers can visit the many shipwrecks and artificial reef sites surrounding the islands or comb the reef surfaces and vertical reef walls.

The seas here are warm all year, supporting vast numbers of fish, urchins, and starfish. Coral reefs just offshore offer shelter to squirrel fish and huge shoals of snapper. The deep ocean channels that cut between and

> **Virgin Islanders claim African, French, Puerto Rican, East Indian, British, Danish, and American roots—among others—in this Caribbean melting pot.**

around certain islands (Pillsbury Sound, for example, between St. Thomas and St. John) are a migratory thoroughfare for a number of large fish and marine mammal species. This offers excitement not only to divers, but also to fishermen; the number of large fish species, including record-breaking marlin, provides some of the most challenging game fishing in the world.

The Virgin Islands has something for everyone, from the bustle of St. Thomas to the natural beauty of St. John, and from the laid-back West Indian flair on Tortola to the unique rock formations at the Baths on Virgin Gorda. There is enough water to sail, dive, or fish to your heart's content. Whatever type of vacation you choose, you'll find your wishes granted several-fold as you are seduced by the spell of the Virgin Islands. The British call them "nature's little secrets," and for the moment they still are.

A BRIEF HISTORY

Although the Virgin Islands today are a tranquil, safe vacation spot, they have had a traumatic and frequently violent history as various colonial powers fought for control. Europe's interest in the Virgin Islands began when Christopher Columbus spotted them in November 1493 on his second voyage to the Caribbean. His fleet was short of potable water, and he sailed toward what is now St. Croix, having found what looked like a safe inlet (the Salt River) where he could send a scouting party to search for the needed supplies. Unfortunately for him and his men, the land was already occupied by Carib Indians, the tribe that had migrated from the northern coast of South America through the islands and waters now bearing its name.

The Carib were in no mood to let Columbus have his way, and a bloody skirmish ensued. Columbus left quickly and headed west to Puerto Rico, but not before naming the islands "Santa Ursula y Las Once Mil Vírgenes" after St. Ursula (who was martyred for her Christian beliefs) and her 11,000 virgin acolytes. He also gave the name "Santa Cruz" to the island he first sighted.

Face from the past: wood-carving depicting a conquistador, Virgin Gorda.

The Carib were themselves relative newcomers, having arrived to take the islands by force from other native peoples only about a hundred years before Columbus. Before them, Arawak tribes such as the Taino had settled many islands in the area around A.D. 200 and lived simple, peaceful lives. Their weaving and pottery skills were highly developed; it was the Arawak who gave the world the hammock, which provides so much relaxation on the islands today. And much earlier there had been a group known as the Ciboney, who were living on St. Thomas around 3,000 years ago.

A ruined sugar mill attests to Tortola's far-from-sweet history of slave labor.

The Beginnings of European Rule

The Ciboney, Arawak, and Carib peoples obviously found the Virgin Islands a desirable place to live. The Spanish, however, were more interested in the gold and treasure to be found in South America and thus never settled the islands that had been claimed for the Spanish crown. They nevertheless used the native population as a slave labor force to work in the mines, and many were shipped off to Hispaniola and other Spanish strongholds. By the beginning of the 17th century the native population had been so decimated by disease and forced labor that there were virtually no Indians left.

Historical Landmarks

ca. A.D. 200   Arawak Indians travel north and settle throughout the Caribbean, displacing the Ciboney.

ca. 1300   Carib tribes drive out the Arawak.

1493   Columbus names the islands and claims them for Spain.

1500–1650   Pirates keep control of the waters around the Virgin Islands.

1650–1665   Colonial powers (French, Dutch, English, and Spanish) fight over control of the islands.

1672   Tortola becomes British; St. Thomas is settled by Danish newcomers.

1733   A successful slave revolt in St. John lasts 6 months, but is then put down by French forces; St. Croix is sold to the Danish West India Company.

1834   Britain declares the slave trade illegal.

1838   Full emancipation; ex-slaves take over land from planter families who have left the islands.

1848   Slavery ends in the Danish islands.

1878   The burning of Frederiksted on St. Croix in a mass social uprising.

1917   The Danish West Indian Islands are bought by the United States for $25 million in gold, becoming the US Virgin Islands.

1956   Laurance Rockefeller buys large tracts of land on St. John and donates it to the US government. The British Virgin Islands are created as a colony.

1966   Queen Elizabeth II makes an official visit to the British Virgin Islands, which receive a new constitution the following year.

1989   Hurricane Hugo rips through the Virgin Islands, resulting in terrible damage.

1996   Official annexation of Water Island to the USVI

Neighboring islands, though ostensibly Spanish, had no organized settlements or rule of law, and their prime location so close to the main shipping lanes for the Spanish fleet made them an ideal hideout for pirates waiting to raid the treasure galleons. Each cut-throat gang had its own hideaway complete with food and rum supplies. Hoards of their captured booty are said to remain hidden in the remote coves of the Virgin Islands, but nobody has yet found any traces.

In 1625 St. Croix (at that time called "Santa Cruz," its Spanish equivalent) was settled by both the English and the Dutch, beginning over a century of warfare and rivalry that mirrored the power struggles taking place in Europe. The English prevailed over the Spanish on Santa Cruz and kept the island until 1650, when Spain retook it. Seeing an opportunity to regain the island, the Dutch immediately attacked but were unsuccessful. It was the French who eventually came along and wrested the island from the Spanish grip.

The English and Dutch were also fighting over Tortola, but this was a battle the English won in 1672, and Tortola has remained under the Union Jack since then, giving Britain a strong base in the Caribbean.

St. Croix continued to be a pawn in the power game. It passed to the Knights of Malta, who promptly gave it the French name we know today. They were not impressed by their new base and at one point burned all the vegetation in a rather extreme attempt to rid the island of mosquitoes. When the French West India Company bought St. Croix in 1665, its directors found that the ashy residue of the fires was the perfect soil nutrient and promptly began large-scale cultivation of sugar cane. They also introduced slavery, the practice that made production of sugar's byproducts— molasses and rum—profitable. The British did the same on Tortola, and the region became extremely wealthy.

The last of the major islands to be colonized was St. Thomas, which had been a major pirate stronghold with Francis Drake acting under a royal warrant as "Pirate to the Queen." In May 1672, 91 Danish and Norwegian colonists set foot on St. Thomas with a royal charter from King Christian V to develop the Danish West India and Guinea Company. The town they founded was named after King Christian's wife, Charlotte Amalie. St. Thomas was too hilly to support itself solely through agriculture, so the natural harbor of Charlotte Amalie was developed as a trading port and the main slave market for the area. Trade with the colonies, Europe, and the African coast was extremely successful and was further enhanced when St. Thomas was declared a free port in 1724, a status it retains today.

Danish settlers made the short trip across Pillsbury Sound to settle on St. John in 1717. Within a few years there were over one hundred plantations on the island, but a shocking and bloody slave revolt in 1733 brought the system to a sudden halt. The Danish settlers and a British contingent sent to help them were all slaughtered, and the slaves declared a free community. Such an act sent shudders through the other colonies

The Knighted Pirate

Sir Francis Drake is one of the heroes of British history. As a seafaring explorer, he sailed around the world from 1577 to 1580. Later, when the Spanish fleet threatened the English coast in 1588, he led the English Navy to a famous victory. For this he was given a knighthood by Elizabeth I.

He was, however, also a pirate and privateer who plied the waters of the northern Caribbean from his base in the Virgin Islands, taking treasure from Spanish galleons and attacking Spanish ports. He led successful raids on Hispaniola and on St. Augustine in Florida.

in the Caribbean. The authorities could not allow this oasis of freedom to remain in the midst of other slave islands, and a French force was dispatched to quell the rebellion. They did a thorough job, killing as many rebels as they found; many rebels chose to commit suicide rather than face the wrath of the soldiers. In the end not one of the rebel slaves survived.

In the same year, France sold St. Croix to the Danish West India Company. In spite of the rebellion across the water on St. John, there was no shortage of Europeans wanting to buy plots of land to start new plantations. The Danes made St. Thomas a crown colony and the capital of their Danish West Indies, a collection of three islands.

As Britain and France fought in Europe in the middle of the 18th century, their war spilled over into the Caribbean. The Danes stayed neutral, and Charlotte Amalie became the busiest "safe" port in the region, reaping the benefits of their neighbors' squabbles. The Danes decided to move their capital to Christiansted on St. Croix, principally because its buildings did not have thatched roofs and thus posed less of a fire risk.

Emancipation and Economic Downturns

St. Croix continued to prosper, and in 1800 more than half the island was under sugar cane cultivation, with 27,000 slaves supporting the industry. However, the tide was turning against the use of slaves, and Denmark was at the forefront of the movement. Fortunately for the planters, the British (who were not yet opposed to slavery) decided to take St. Croix in 1801 as a strategic buffer during the Napoleonic Wars. But Denmark retook control after only ten months, thereafter promptly banning the trade in slaves— the first step in banning slavery altogether. Although the British returned between 1807 and 1815, the trade in slaves remained illegal and plantation life began to lose its rosy glow for the planters. At the same time, sugar beets began to break the monopoly of the cane growers, and economic collapse loomed for planters throughout the Virgin Islands.

In 1834 slavery was abolished on British islands. A 4-year period of transition followed during which the former slaves endured an "apprenticeship", working the same jobs as before. Complete emancipation came in 1838. On Tortola, Virgin Gorda, and Jost Van Dyke, most of the planters cut their losses, sold (or simply gave) their land to the former slaves, and headed for the motherland. Thus the great majority of today's residents of the British Virgin Islands own their own homes and land, passed down since emancipation through the generations. The Danish Virgin Islands finally buckled under the growing pressure in 1848, with the formal emancipation proclamation delivered by Governor-General Peter von Scholten to avert a violent rebellion. However, land in the Danish colonies remained in the hands of the wealthy few.

Unfortunately, freedom did not mean health, wealth, and happiness. In the 1850s and 1860s, four cholera epidemics struck the region. St. Croix was spared, only to be hit by drought and hurricanes. As the economic situation worsened, rioting erupted and climaxed in 1878 with a "fire burn" in Frederiksted, the second town of St. Croix. Half the town and many plantations were destroyed. In St. Thomas, economic troubles were temporarily reversed during the American Civil War, when illicit trade brought about a miniboom that ended abruptly with the Confederate defeat.

Political Change

This decline changed with the onset of World War I, when the US Navy saw the strategic importance of the islands in protecting the Western Hemisphere from possible German incursions. The crucial region guarded the Anegada Passage,

For a splendid example of Danish colonial design, stop by the greathouse at the Estate Whim Plantation Museum.

which links the Caribbean and the Atlantic, and served also as protection for the Panama Canal. The Navy also coveted Charlotte Amalie's harbor as a base for its fleet. The US government offered $25 million for some 25 islands, and (after 245 years) the Danish West Indies became the United States Virgin Islands in 1917.

The US Navy administered the islands for fourteen years, during which little changed for the inhabitants. The land was still poor, and the one major profitable industry—rum—suffered greatly during the American Prohibition in the 1920s. The islands then passed to the auspices of the US Department of the Interior. Islanders themselves were not granted the vote until the Organic Act of 1936; a second act was passed in 1954, allowing for more political autonomy.

As it had for centuries, St. Thomas remained a trading island, but a different fate awaited St. John. The wealthy Rockefeller family saw the benefit of a paradise getaway, complete with exclusive resort hotels, for their well-heeled friends. In 1955 Laurance Rockefeller masterminded the creation of the Caneel Bay Resort, arguably the best hotel in the world at the time. He also foresaw the damage that tourism could inflict on a place, especially one with an ecosystem as delicate as St. John's. In 1956 Rockefeller purchased large portions of the island and deeded them to the US National Park Service. Today, over-development is prohibited, making St. John a natural haven.

In 1956 the British Virgin Islands became a separate colony under the British flag. Queen Elizabeth II visited in 1966, the first visit by a reigning monarch to these distant islands. Her visit also heralded the introduction of a new constitution that granted greater autonomy for the BVI. The day-to-day activities of the islands are overseen by the Legislative Council, and local elections are held every four years. That is not to say the BVI want autonomy. The population of these secure islands seem content with the latest arrangements.

The US Virgin islands were polled in 1993 with regard to their preferred relationship to the United States. Over 80 percent of Virgin Islanders voted to maintain the status quo, while only 4 percent voted for independence.

Tourism, Development, and the Future

All the Virgin Islands have benefited from tourism, a new yet profitable industry. But each has capitalized in its own unique fashion. The trade of St. Thomas is in tax-free "luxury" goods, and its harbor now brings in thousands of cruise ship passengers each week. St. John revels in its natural and protected beauty, St. Croix in its history and its Danish-American feel. The British Virgin Islands have been turned into a sailing paradise through the work of one man, Charlie Cary, who saw the opportunity to develop boating in the islands and built a fleet that has given birth to a full-scale industry.

Although tourism remains "king", other industries also have an impact on the society's economy. In 1965 the Senate of the US Virgin Islands granted the Hess Oil Company a permit to build an oil refinery on the south coast of St. Croix. Today it is the largest refinery in the Western hemisphere and the second largest in the world, employing a significant percentage of the island's population. Tortola has taken a different route, marketing itself as a safe, stable, and extremely successful offshore banking center, especially since Britain handed Hong Kong back to the Chinese in 1997.

This increased wealth has brought problems to the islands as well as benefits. All of the Virgin Islands have thrived since the 1950s in a way not seen since the peak of sugar cane production. This economic boom has attracted migrant workers from less-developed islands throughout the Caribbean. On many Virgin Islands (both US and British), the indigenous population is far outnumbered by foreign workers, threatening to change the balance of this delicate society.

A study in 1992 showed St. Thomas and St. John to be the

Robinson Crusoe, perhaps? If it is, he's found the perfect new home in Anegada.

second most expensive places in the US to live, behind New York City. St. Croix was third. This places an economic burden on the local population, which must earn far more to afford housing and food than do other US residents. Islanders are working hard to make sure that money made from tourism stays in the islands. An example is the casino developments on St. Croix, which will have a majority local ownership.

Although devastated by hurricanes in the latter part of the 20th century—particularly Hugo in 1989 and Marilyn in 1995—the outlook looks rosy. The hope is that the increasing numbers of visitors will not change the essence of these islands. The key is to balance the tourist boom with the ecological and social pressures that success inevitably brings.

Tax-free shopping and exquisite natural beauty make Charlotte Amalie a favorite port of call for the cruise lines.

WHERE TO GO

Although Christopher Columbus quite grandly thought he had discovered 11,000 islands, the Virgin Islands actually number around 100—many of which are unpopulated. Today they comprise two political entities, namely, the United States Virgin Islands and the British Virgin Islands. The US territory has about 102,000 residents on approximately 50 tiny islands and the three main islands of St. Thomas, St. John, and St. Croix. In contrast, the British Virgin Islands is a territory with a population of almost 20,000 living on 36 islands, among which are the four main islands: Tortola, Virgin Gorda, Jost Van Dyke, and Anegada.

THE UNITED STATES VIRGIN ISLANDS

Touches of "Americana" combine with Caribbean flair on the three United States Virgin Islands (USVI). Each one is different from its neighbor, but they all feature the beaches, watersports, and tax-free shopping that make them popular destinations for vacationers. St. Thomas is the free-port and thus the economic and political center. St. John is a major destination for the eco-tourism crowd. And St. Croix boasts every activity involved in the typical Caribbean holiday. A few years ago, the USVI annexed Water Island, a fourth principal island that is only about a mile long. It lies offshore from Charlotte Amalie and was once a World War II military base. The USVI are officially an unincorporated American territory, headed by their own governor and senate and covered by US laws.

St. Thomas

The shopping center of the Caribbean, **St. Thomas** is the most densely populated of the Virgin Islands, with more than 48,000 residents occupying 32 sq miles (82 sq km). It also plays host to the most visitors. Whether it is couples on their honeymoon or families out for fun—or the thousands of cruise ship passengers who arrive in their floating hotels for a whirlwind daytrip—St. Thomas has become a must-visit island for many tourists. As the most American of the three USVI it is the one that will feel most like home for visitors from North America.

Charlotte Amalie

The capital of St. Thomas is **Charlotte Amalie** (pronounced "a-mah´-lya"), which sits on one of the finest natural harbors in the world. The town, named by Danish settlers after the wife of King Christian V, began life as a trading port. Today, it is a successful commercial center. The downtown area, resting between the hills and the harbor, is a maze of old streets and pretty red roofs best seen from the surrounding hills.

Warehouses built along the waterfront by Danish traders in the 17th and 18th centuries still host hundreds of traders. But now, instead of staple goods such as cotton, flour, or salt, the stores are filled with gold, gems, watches, and designer goods. Prices in this tax-free haven are up to 60 percent below prices back home, so make sure that you have room on your credit card for a few bargains.

Shoppers get down to business on Dronningen's Gade, Charlotte Amalie.

The main shopping streets lie close to the harbor between Veteran's Drive and Dronningen's Gade. A series of narrow alleys between these two streets are filled with craft, clothing, and jewelry shops along with cafés and restaurants.

But Charlotte Amalie is not just a shoppers' paradise. There are cultural attractions here, and some historic gems to be discovered. Perhaps the most important of the latter is **Fort Christian**, east of downtown. Work on the fort began in 1671 to protect the harbor and the valuable cargo that docked at the quayside. It was the only permanent structure in the town for many years; homes were little more than simple thatched huts with wooden walls. (None survive today due to a series of fires that swept the town, the worst occurring in 1831.) The terra-cotta walls, painted shutters, and crenelated clock tower give the building a cozy rather than a military look. The fort today has been transformed into a museum of US Virgin Islands life, with rotating exhibits of colonial furniture, archives, and old photographs of the islands and their inhabitants. Take a walk outside on the fort's walls for a wonderful view over the seafront of Charlotte Amalie and the colorful **Vendors Plaza**, a craft market under bright parasols, which has a permanent home in the fort's shadow.

> Use "Good morning," "Good afternoon," or "Good evening" when beginning conversations with taxi drivers, shop assistants, and anyone giving you directions.

Next to the fort is the picturesque **Legislature Building**, with its classical façade painted lime green. The building, finished in 1874, was used as a barracks for troops based at the fort. Sessions of the USVI Senate take place here and are open to the public. You can also take a tour of the building's interior.

Behind the fort and the Vendors Plaza is **Emancipation Park**, perhaps the best place in town to sit in the shade of the

Charlotte Amalie's Fort Christian, dating back to 1671, is a historical gem and an important museum.

trees and enjoy the cooling sea breeze after sightseeing and shopping. The park was named to commemorate the freeing of the slaves in 1848. Around it are some important sites for visitors. Across Tolbod Gade is the tourist information office, where you can pick up maps and other information, and on the park's northwest corner is the main post office.

Make your way there, but don't be tempted to turn right and head for the stores just yet. Take a left onto Norre Gade and travel past the Grand Hotel—once the finest hotel in Charlotte Amalie and now converted into offices and shops—to visit the **Lutheran Church**, which will be on your left. Built in 1820, it is still regularly used for services and has a wonderful sweeping staircase leading to the entrance.

Take the stairway to Kongens Gade, the street behind the Lutheran Church. These steps climb a steep hill that houses many of the oldest and most important buildings of Danish-era Charlotte Amalie. While the warehouses sat on the quayside, the family houses of the merchants and civil servants were built high on **Government Hill** to take advantage of the cooling breezes. Kongens Gade itself has several buildings that date back to the late 18th and early 19th centuries. **Hotel 1829** (named for the year it was built) is today one of the most unusual hotels on St. Thomas. Behind this building are Galleon House and Lavalette House, both shaded by mature trees. Pass Hotel 1829 and pause at the steps beside it, which climb higher up Government Hill. These are the "**99 Steps**," one of a series of urban stairways built by the Danes in the mid-1700s to allow pedestrian access to the town below. The Steps are the longest stairway in town, but whoever named it must have become tired toward the end and miscounted; there are in fact 103.

Walking farther along Kongens Gade, past the Lutheran Parsonage erected in 1725, brings you to **Government House**, an archetypal colonial mansion with an ornate wrought-iron balcony. The building, which is now the office for the Governor of the USVI, was constructed in 1867 and originally used for meetings of the Danish Colonial Council. The grand house was totally

Don't miss St. Thomas's 99 Steps. And count while you go—there are actually 103.

renovated in 1974. As Kongens Gade begins to drop once again down the far side of Government Hill, you will pass Moron House and the Lieutenant Governor's Office. Take a left turn down the small alley next to the office to reach **Seven Arches House Museum**, once the home of a Danish master craftsman. The house has a "welcoming arms" staircase (fashionable in the 18th century) leading to the entrance, supported by brick arches reminiscent of the streets of Christiansted on St. Croix. Completely restored and filled with period furniture, the museum is a step back in time. The upper floor also has wonderful views over the harbor and town. Be sure to watch for the iguanas that call the surrounding gardens home.

Take the 99 Steps to the summit of Government Hill. At the top is **Haagensen House**, another renovated period property. Its original owner, Hans Haagensen, was a Danish banker. The remains of **Blackbeard's Castle**, thought to be the home of the famous pirate Edward Teach, are also here. The streets on Government Hill boast more colonial homes, including Crown House, which was once the Governor's mansion. (Those who don't want to climb the steps can take a shuttle to Haagensen House from the Pampered Pirate gift shop on Norre Gade.)

From Ballast to Buildings

The warehouses of Charlotte Amalie and Christiansted, along with the forts built by the Danes, were constructed of bricks. But there are no brick works in the islands. The bricks came from Europe on empty trading ships, acting as ballast to keep the ships stable. When the boats arrived in the islands, they unloaded the bricks and filled up with cargoes of rum and sugar for the journey home. The bricks were then used for construction, and the settlers were assured a steady supply. The thick walls and low profiles of the buildings also gave then a strong resistance against hurricanes.

One of the most beautiful and unusual buildings in Charlotte Amalie is the **St. Thomas Synagogue** (located on Crystal Gade), the oldest synagogue building still in use under the American flag. The Jewish community here has always been strong, even from the very earliest days of Danish settlement in 1655. When Charlotte Amalie suffered the large fire of 1831, there were 64 families worshipping in the small synagogue; only one sacred Torah scroll could be saved before flames destroyed the building. The present structure was built on the same spot and opened in 1833, made

Government House, where the governor of the USVI keeps his offices.

hurricane-proof with local pine and ballast bricks from Danish cargo ships. The sand on the synagogue floor is said to be symbolic of Israel's flight from Egypt.

Even back down on the main shopping street (Dronningen's Gade), there are snippets of history. A tiny sign pointing down a dim alley directs you to **Pissarro House**, at number 14. This is the birthplace of Camille Pissarro, father of the Impressionist school of painting. Born here in 1830, Pissarro moved to Paris, where he formed close ties to Monet and Renoir and in the 1870s worked with Cézanne. There is little in the house to indicate Pissarro's presence: it is now a commercial gallery that displays the work of up-and-coming international and

Pissarro House, birthplace of the father of Impressionism, Camille Pissarro, showcases local and international talent.

local artists. But the gallery's owner is immensely knowledgeable about Pissarro, the man, and his work.

The market square, farther west, is located at the site of the old slave market. You can find fruit and vegetables for sale here, but come early in the morning. Saturday is the best day.

The waterfront plays an important part in Charlotte Amalie's economic life. Ferry boats to St. John and Tortola and hydrofoils to St. Croix leave from here. Sea planes depart for flights or for sightseeing tours across St. Thomas, St. John, and a host of British islands (see page 82). Numerous boats also deliver commercial cargo. Just offshore are two islands, Hassel and Water, both used by the US Navy during World War II. **Water Island** is now open to visitors who want to explore this natural haven just minutes away from the bustle of town.

The cruise port is situated at the **West India Company Dock**, a mile east of town—a pleasant 30-minute walk around the harbor. Those who want to ride will find taxis waiting to take them to and from Charlotte Amalie. The dock can accommodate three large cruise ships or several smaller vessels, making it one of the largest in the Caribbean. Old Danish warehouses have been transformed into **Havensight Shopping Mall**, which has over 80 tax-free boutiques plus cafés, restaurants, a tourist information office, an ATM, bank facilities, and a post office, all only a few steps away from the huge ships.

Here you'll also find the ticket office for the **Atlantis Submarine**. The mini-submarine, seating around 30 passengers, dives some 60 ft (18 m) under the sea to view coral reefs and the marine life around them. A ferry takes you out to Buck Island, 3 miles (5 km) offshore, to rendezvous with the sub, which then submerges to spend about 50 minutes exploring the reef around the island. Shoals of yellow-tailed snapper surround the craft, looking in as you look out. You might also see sharks, rays, and turtles. The ride is great fun for young and old alike and a safe way to see the underwater world.

Alongside the cruise port is **Flag Hill**, rising over 700 ft (213 m) above sea level and offering panoramic views over Charlotte Amalie and its surrounding hills and harbor. The

---

A Month of Revolutionary Celebrations

St. Thomas awakens to the sound of parties on 14 July each year, when a small area just west of Charlotte Amalie comes alive to celebrate Bastille Day. This is Frenchtown, home to the descendants of settlers who traveled from the French island of St. Barthélemy several generations ago and who still enjoy marking the start of the French Revolution of 1789 as much as they do in Paris. Of course, being a US territory, St. Thomas celebrates the 4th of July as well as the 14th.

☞ **Paradise Point Tramway** carries passengers to a platform at the top for the view, and there is a café-bar if you want to stop for refreshment.

Around St. Thomas

Like most of the other Virgin Islands, St. Thomas is full of hills, and the roads twist and turn around sharp bends. Attractions are not well marked, so take care, but you won't get hopelessly lost on such a small island.

Taking the coast road west out of Charlotte Amalie leads to Cyril E. King Airport, but not before you pass a series of wooden pastel houses set in neat rows. This is **Frenchtown**,

Scared of SCUBA? In the Atlantis Submarine, you can explore the ocean depths without getting your feet wet.

home to a community of families who arrived here generations ago from St. Barthélemy, farther south in the Caribbean. They still retain their traditions and their Gallic cuisine. Beyond the airport the island becomes less densely populated. Here you'll find the campus of the **University of the Virgin Islands** (founded in 1962), set in an attractive hillside location near Brewers Bay; there is a sister campus on St. Croix.

To see the main attractions of St. Thomas it's better to head directly north up into the hills behind Charlotte Amalie. Take Malfolie Road (Route 35) out of town and climb the hill past the Malfolie Hotel and Restaurant. The views back toward Charlotte Amalie are quite beautiful.

At the top of the hill take a left at Route 40 and stop at the roadside turnout about 1 km (½ mile) farther along. This is **Drake's Seat**, your first panoramic view of the northern coast-

Idyllic, heart-shaped Magen's Bay, where locals and visitors alike flock for some fun in the sun.

line, the neighboring island of Tortola, and Magen's Bay directly below—probably the best beach on St. Thomas and one of the most famous in the Caribbean. There is also a view of the peninsula sheltering Magen's Bay, Peterborg, where President William J. Clinton spent a family holiday in 1998. Drake's Seat is supposedly where Francis Drake watched ships traveling west through the sea passage that now bears his name. Today you share the view with T-shirt and refreshment vendors.

Continue along Route 40 to reach **Estate St. Peter Greathouse and Botanical Gardens**, on 11 acres (4½ hectares) along the ridge near the summit of St. Peter Peak. Established in the 19th century, it was owned in the 1930s by Virgin Islands Governor Lawrence Cramer. Both the house and the gardens were totally destroyed by Hurricane Hugo in 1989.

Only the chimney of the greathouse was left standing after the storm, and the gardens were totally washed away. Today the house and gardens have been restored and developed to combine history with modern amenities. An observation deck around the house is the perfect place to see the views to the south, and there is a nature trail through the garden.

Route 33 (off Route 40) leads to **Mountain Top**, which at 1547 ft (472 m) offers a better view than does Drake's Seat, particularly down to Magen's Bay. There is a sophisticated shopping mall and a large bar area with almost nonstop daiquiris (they claim to have invented the banana daiquiri here). Because everyone comes with a camera, you might have to wait a while to see the view for yourself.

Magen's Bay is a "heart-shaped" stretch of sand. The beach and trees are designated as a public park, but you pay a small fee to enter the beach area. Because it is so sheltered from sea swells and currents, it is a safe place for children to swim and for everyone to snorkel, although it can be very busy.

> Never wear beach clothing in towns or shopping areas. Bare chests for men and bare midriffs for women are considered improper.

Climb up out of Magen's Bay and take Route 42 to Route 38 in order to reach the eastern part of St. Thomas. Here you will find beautiful coves where many of the large resort hotels have been built. Look out for the turnoff to **Coki Point**, where there is a pleasant sandy beach and a number of craft stalls. At the end of the point is **Coral World**, an attraction offering a fascinating look at life under the water. It is built around a number of controlled marine environments, each with its own animals or fish. Look for the stingray, shark, and turtle pools, where regular feeding times are posted. You'll even get a chance to pet some of the creatures. Pride of place at Coral World must go to the genuine coral reef that has been embedded in the open water offshore. An underground viewing area reached via a walkway allows you to watch the daily activity of the reef fish and some of the larger wild creatures who come for the free food provided by Coral World staff.

Snorkeling offshore at Coki Beach is popular because of the quantity of sea creatures attracted by the regular feedings at Coral World. The water can get busy because many of the cruise ships send passengers here for snorkeling, but you are almost always guaranteed a good show of marine life.

At the eastern end of St. Thomas is the town of **Red Hook**. This is the island's major sailing centre, with a commercial ferry dock sending boats to St. John and Tortola. Red Hook comes alive in the evening, when hotel guests take the brief taxi trip into town to visit several good restaurants and bars.

Want to watch sharks at dinner time? At Coral World you can safely view the frenzy from the underwater observatory.

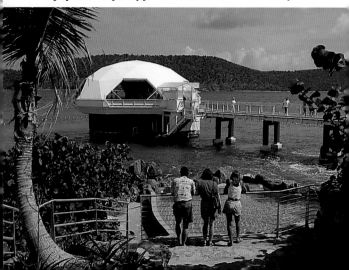

After Red Hook it is a short ride around the southeastern coastline back to Charlotte Amalie. Here you will find a number of beaches such as Limetree and Morningstar—where you can rent a chair for the day and simply do nothing.

St. John

A 30-minute ferry ride of 4 miles (6½ km) across **Pillsbury Sound** takes you from St. Thomas to **St. John**, the smallest of the major US Virgin Islands and one of the most natural islands in the whole Caribbean. St. John is 19 sq miles (50 sq km) of volcanic hills, two-thirds of which is designated as the United States Virgin Islands National Park, which has protected the natural flora and fauna since 1956. This gives St. John a tranquillity and beauty that has been lost on other islands in the rush to develop and modernize. The population of nearly 4,000 fully support the protection process and today work hard to preserve the pristine sandy beaches and nature trails, making St. John one of the world's prime destinations for the environmentally conscious traveler.

Cruz Bay

Cruz Bay is the small capital of St. John and home to the majority of its permanent residents. Commercial ferries dock at a tiny passenger jetty a few paces from town, which consists of a few streets full of bars, restaurants, and shops. A park stands behind the passenger jetty, with shady seats and a bust marking the emancipation of slaves on the island. Nearby is an information stand that provides a little information about the national park and a list of weekly activities of interest to visitors.

You can spend a few hours browsing in the malls. But if you're not in a shopping mood, a trip around town could take as little as 30 minutes. Cruz Bay really comes alive at night, when people come into town—after a day on the beach or a

Commercial ferries line the town wharf at Cruz Bay, the small capital of St. John.

hike in the forest—to enjoy a beer or two and maybe a daiquiri before a pleasant dinner. Live music floats through the air from a dozen places around town, and there's always a good spot for some toe tapping or a sing-along.

Walking to the left from the passenger jetty along the waterfront brings you to the national park office. Behind this is a tourist office in a tiny wooden building, where you can find maps and information, and next door is a post office. Opposite these three buildings, beyond a small car park, is the customs dock and office. This is the port of entry for non-Americans arriving by sailboat or motor launch and the port of re-entry for Americans who have traveled across to Jost Van Dyke or Tortola (in the British Virgin Islands) for the day. If you have booked an excursion with a private company, however, they will take care of all the simple formalities.

Continue your walk around the waterfront and dock area. Just as you begin to think that you are leaving town,

Mongoose Junction shopping mall will appear on the right, named after the critters that used to congregate on the spot before the mall was built. Here you will be able to shop for local arts, crafts, clothing, jewelry, and refreshments.

A right at the passenger dock leads to the **Wharfside Village** mall. The white wooden building, bedecked with bougainvillaea, houses a number of boutiques, bars, and restaurants.

Around St. John

For most visitors, St. John is not about nightlife or shopping. Instead, the lure is the broad expanse of unspoiled vegetation, some of the best beaches in the world, and the rocks and reefs, home to myriad species of marine life. The island is small, so you can rent a vehicle and see it all in a day. The road system is simple, but many sections of the USVI National Park are accessible only by foot, and some remote bays and coves are known only to sailors. Another option is to get a taxi at the ferry terminal to take you on a tour; fares are clearly listed.

Travel north out of Cruz Bay on North Shore Road (Route 20), a series of rollercoaster dips with some sharp bends. This road leads to the beautiful, pristine beaches

Sundown in Cruz Bay is right about when the town starts coming to life.

for which St. John is rightly famed. A whole string of **beaches** lie tucked away in bays here, and you will find views to grace the best travel magazine covers. Verdant forest hugging the road cools your journey. Out across the water there are off-shore cays (small islands), and the British island of Jost Van Dyke in the distance. The panorama from each headland vies for the title "Best View in the Virgin Islands."

Over the hill beyond Cruz Bay, after driving a few minutes, you will find **Caneel Bay** and Caneel Bay Plantation Resort, one of the most exclusive hotels in the Caribbean. Guests here enjoy seven beautiful beaches and amazing snorkeling areas offshore. Many small boats anchor here to take advantage of the underwater rocks and reefs. Beyond Caneel Bay is **Hawksnest Bay**, and just before the road drops down to the beach there is a dramatic view from the bluff above. You can stop to photograph the beach and the bay with a view of some of the British Virgin Islands in the background.

> Much of St. John is taken up by the USVI National Park. You will enter it frequently as you drive through the island.

Next comes **Trunk Bay**, with a fine beach that can get crowded when a cruise ship buses passengers in for the morning. Trunk Bay is world renowned for its guided snorkeling tour around two rocks lying a few yards offshore. Even novice snorkelers can enjoy the underwater world in the pristine Virgin Islands water, where information signs point out items of interest along the 656-ft (200-m) tour. Lifeguards stationed at the beach watch out for anyone who gets into trouble.

Trunk Bay is said to be named after the trunkback (or leatherback) turtle, which uses St. John and other Virgin Islands as a breeding ground. If you watch the water carefully you might see a small turtle head come up for air before disappearing underwater once again. Divers in the deeper water offshore report greater numbers in recent years, and turtle eggs are protected by national park staff in an effort to improve their numbers.

Next to Trunk Bay is **Cinnamon Bay**, a beautiful beach and one of two campgrounds in the national park (the other is at Maho Bay). The campsite, directly on the beach, is the starting point for a number of hiking trails through the inland forest. Hikes here last from a few hours to a full day. Iguanas, pelicans, and frigate birds can all be enjoyed in their natural environment, as can the wild asses that were introduced to the island as pack animals and now roam the hillsides, sometimes raiding campsites at night. The Cinnamon Bay campsite is one of the most popular in the world, and demand for the limited space is high. Be sure to book well in advance (park staff recommend a full year; see page 113).

Coastguard on the lookout: a pelican keeps his eye on the action from his roost.

You don't need to stay at the camp to enjoy Cinnamon Beach, a long ribbon of sand with a shop selling drinks. In recent years the beach has been eroding back into the bay, which is threatening the **Taino Indian Ceremonial Site**. Experts date the site to the time of Columbus in the late 15th century, when the area was populated by the Taino, an Arawak tribe.

Swimmers and sunbathers now share the area with a team of archaeologists carefully extracting as much evidence of native life as possible. Many simple offerings have been unearthed here, including large shells and clay figures.

Beyond Cinnamon Bay are **Maho Bay** and **Francis Bay**, both exquisite sites for a day of relaxation. Because they are farther from Cruz Bay they tend to be a bit less crowded, but the beaches and water are just as impressive. Maho Bay environmental campground, the second campsite connected with the national park, is located in the acres of forest behind the beach. It was created using as many eco-friendly systems and policies as possible.

From Maho Bay the road leads away from the coast. There is a sign to the left for **Annaberg Sugar Plantation**, which sits

History and nature combine to form a spectacular walk through the Annaberg Sugar Plantation ruins, St. John.

on a forested hillside above **Leinster Bay**. The plantation was once one of the largest in the Virgin Islands, and the remains of its windmill and refining area can still be seen. There are also clear views across to Tortola and the offshore islands of Great Thatch and Little Thatch in the British Virgin Islands. The **Annaberg Sugar Plantation Ruins Walk** is one of the most picturesque trails through the Virgin Islands National Park.

Return back to Route 20 and travel inland until you find Center Line Road. This is the main road running along the interior spine of the island, linking Cruz Bay in the west with Coral Bay, the major settlement in the east of the island. The land in the eastern part of St. John is much flatter than in the west; this was the area first settled by the Danes because it was much easier to grow crops and sugar cane.

Coral Bay was the largest early settlement on St. John, home to the 1733 rebellion in which slaves held the island for six months. Eventually the rebellion was quelled by French troops and all the rebels perished. The plantation system never recovered from the rebellion, and many planters moved to St. Croix to start a new life. Today Coral Bay is a small, relaxed town. Its harbor is a favorite with charter sailors. Life is a little quiet, which is how most local people want to keep it.

Next to Coral Bay is **Hurricane Hole**, the bay preferred by many as refuge when there is a risk of severe storm or hurricane. The mountains to the west normally divert the worst of the prevailing winds, offering a little more peace of mind than does the open water.

Head back along Center Line Road for a direct route back to Cruz Bay. Outside Coral Bay, the road climbs high into the hills and through the heart of the national park. Stop at Le Chateau de Bordeaux restaurant, where **Bordeaux Mountain**, the highest point on St. John at 1300 ft (396 m), is just a little to your right. Look back toward Coral Bay for a wonderful

Looking for some peace and quiet? The serene beauty of Coral Bay will not disappoint.

panorama as the British Virgin Islands lay out before you. Try to do this in the afternoon, when the sun is behind you and the islands can be seen more clearly. If you have your own transportation, this is also a good place to stop for dinner.

Just beyond Bordeaux Mountain on the way to Cruz Bay is a sign indicating the **Reef Bay Trail**, which leads to a collection of petroglyphs (rock carvings) deep in the forest. Nobody can tell for sure who carved these—Taino Indians or slaves. All the theories will be fully explained by the ranger guide who accompanies you on the trail. The hike is downhill to the petroglyphs but a stiff 3-mile (5-km) uphill walk on the way back, so the national park has introduced a ferry service for those who want to hike down to Reef Bay and then take a boat back to Cruz Bay. Times and prices are posted on the notice board in the park in Cruz Bay. You must book the guided tour in advance at the national park office near the ferry dock in town.

St. Croix

Lying some 40 miles (64 km) south of St. Thomas and St. John, **St. Croix** is by far the most Caribbean of the three American islands. It is the largest of all the Virgin Islands and has vast areas of untouched land, particularly in the east where the undulating hills and dry scrub could easily be mistaken for Crete in the Mediterranean.

On St. Croix (pronounced "Sin Croy"), there are many more vestiges of the Danish colonial past. In the 17th and 18th centuries, St. Croix was the most developed of the Danish colonies because it was most conducive to plantation development.

Virgin Islands National Park

In the early 1950s, Laurance Rockefeller became concerned about the eventual results of overdevelopment on St. John. The Rockefeller family itself owned local land and commercial interests, but he wanted to limit the negative impact on this beautiful island. His solution was to buy large tracts of virgin forest to donate to the US government. In 1956 President Eisenhower created the US Virgin Islands National Park. Later, a portion of underwater landscape was added to bring the current total protected area to 11,560 acres (4,677 hectares). Nearly two-thirds of St. John's land area is included in the national park.

Here there are over 100 species of trees, numerous animals (iguanas, bats, and mongooses) and birds, and many marine creatures (turtles, rays, and sharks). Some of these are on the verge of extinction yet have a safe habitat in the park. Visitors enjoy 22 nature trails, several beaches, two campsites, and surrounding clear waters where they can enjoy protected interactions with all of nature's creatures.

The old mill and waterfront at Christiansted, capital of St. Croix.

Many large sugar cane plantations were situated on the island and many slaves came to work the land. Today, the remains of historic forts, houses, and windmills can be seen scattered all across St. Croix, and Virgin Islands rum is still produced here. It also has the most complex history of any Virgin Island, because it has been ruled by seven countries during its colonial history. The local population, the Cruzans, reflect this dynamic history, possessing a great sense of self and a love of their island.

The economy of St. Croix is more diverse than on the other Virgin Islands, with industries such as the Hess oil refinery, which occupies a large site on the southern coast. But on an island of 84 sq miles (216 sq km), a visitor can quite easily avoid the factories altogether and search out some of the more seductive delights, of which there are many.

☛ *Christiansted*

Christiansted, the capital of St. Croix, is situated on a reef-sheltered stretch of the northern coastline and filled with reminders of Danish rule. Many of the buildings in the downtown area date from the 17th and 18th centuries; the layout of the town is still a Danish-designed grid system, with a mixture of Danish and English street names. Part of the historic downtown area, restored to its former glory, has been declared a US National Monument.

Perhaps the most striking building in town is **Fort Christiansvaern**, which still dominates the waterfront. The mustard-yellow walls and green shutters are traditional Danish colors, and the effect, especially in the late afternoon sun, is spectacular. The fort was built in 1749 to protect the port and its valuable cargoes from pirates and rival colonial powers. After you have purchased tickets at Scale House nearby, walk though the large gates to explore the interior. Take a look in the gunpowder magazine and the arsenal and then climb the stairs to the walls and take in the vista, little changed since the Danes created the town.

Alongside the fort is a grassy area fronting King's Wharf. Two important buildings can be found here. **Scale House**, built in 1856, was the place where goods such as sugar, rum, and cotton were weighed or counted before they were shipped. The Danish weightmaster, who had an office in the building, was one of the most important men on the island. Although remains of a scale can still be seen in a portion of the ground floor, today the building houses a visitors' bureau, with maps of the historic area and tickets for the fort. The Danish **Customs House**, dating from 1734, sits behind Scale House; it now houses the National Park Service administration offices.

Offshore you can see **Protestant Cay**, a tiny island given its name because Protestants were exiled there during religious conflicts that once paralyzed Europe. Today it has a hotel and small public beach reached by a regular two-minute ferry service.

If you walk away from the waterfront across Hospital Gade (Hospital Street), you'll see a wooden church. This is **Steeple Building**, originally a Lutheran place of worship that was the

With its mustard-colored walls and green shutters, Fort Christiansvaern retains the traditions of Danish design.

first church built by the Danish settlers in 1734; in 1753 it was known as the Church of God of Sabaoth. In the middle of the 18th century, it was taken over by the military and used as a bakery, after which it underwent a number of transformations, becoming first a hospital and then a school. In 1954 the site was incorporated in the historic downtown area and now houses a museum of St. Croix history from Amerindian times to the present day. The post office across Companiers Gade was once the Danish West India Company warehouse, where all imported and exported goods were stored.

The streets behind Scale and Customs houses are much the same now as they were in colonial times. Two-storey brick buildings have colonnaded walkways created to shade pedestrians. These were merchants' houses, where families lived above the company store. Today, although the stores remain at street level, the upper-floor areas are more likely to be converted into bars and restaurants. Wander the cool sidewalks for tax-free shopping opportunities.

Kogens Gade (King Street) is the main thoroughfare of the town. The imposing **Government House** can be found here. Originally a private home for merchant Johan Shopen, it was purchased in 1771 by the Danish West India Company as a house for the Governor-General. The elegant façade, large rooms, and central location only minutes from the port made it an ideal residence for the most important man on St. Croix. In 1794 another house was built next to the Shopen House for merchant Adam Sobotker, and the two buildings were combined in 1826, then remodeled in 1830 to create the structure you see today. In 1999 it had a complete renovation.

North of Kogans Gade, as you head back toward the water of Christiansted Harbor, you'll find several pedestrian walkways filled with shops and bars. The newest is **King's Alley**, which fronts the Seaborne Aviation seaplane dock. The seafront bar brews its own beer. You can also wander along Comanche Walk, Pan Am Pavilion, and Caravelle Arcade. The **St. Croix Aquarium and Marine Education Center**, in

Steeple Building, the first church built by the Danish settlers of Christiansted.

Caravelle Arcade, allows you to take a close-up look at ocean life. Kids will enjoy the shallow pool, where they can pet a number of harmless creatures. The Aquarium is a great educational resource for local schools and the public alike.

Around St. Croix

St. Croix is a large island, so take a few days to savor it. Explore the east end first, then enjoy the delights of the west end. The roads are in good condition, and it is easy to find the major attractions.

The eastern end of St. Croix is dry, and cacti and low scrub cover the ranging hills. It is less populated than the central and western parts of the island. You can travel clockwise from Christiansted on Route 82, which follows the northern coast. Once out of town, you will pass the fine golf course and tennis facilities of the Buccaneer Hotel.

Remnants of a Danish colonial past: Scale House and the old Customs House will take you back in time.

A number of sandy bays come into view here, along with a small island just offshore. **Buck Island** (not to be confused with an even smaller Buck Island off St. Thomas) is said to be one of the best snorkeling environments in the world. The uninhabited island is a safe environment for turtles, coral, fish species, and the rare brown pelican. There are also less-glamorous species, such as hermit crabs, starfish, and sea cucumbers. The island and the surrounding waters, 880 acres (356 hectares) in all, have been declared a protected area: the **Buck Island Reef National Monument**. Well-marked snorkeling trails have been created in the shallows along the eastern side of the island. Several companies offer day sails to the island, where you can swim, sunbathe, snorkel, and have lunch before returning to your hotel. These concessions operate under National Park Service rules: if you intend to take a private boat to the island, contact the National Park Service office at Customs House in Christiansted for a list of regulations.

At the end of Route 82 is **Point Udall**, the easternmost spit of land in the US. Sit on the low wall and feel the wind in your hair as you look out toward the west coast of Africa thousands of miles away. After visiting Point Udall, take Route 60 to travel along the south shore. Rolling countryside fills the landscape, with only a few houses sitting against the seashore. The refurbished Divi Carina Bay Hotel is the major resort on this part of the island, with a new casino (the only one in the Virgin Islands) luring seasonal gamblers and those simply out to try their luck.

Much of the land on the south coast of St. Croix is taken up by the Hess Oil Refinery and the airport, so head back to Christiansted before traveling west. Take Route 70 (also called Centerline Road or Queen Mary Highway), from which three important attractions can be visited. First on the right is **St. George Village Botanical Garden**, set in the ruins of an

As the sign proudly declares, Point Udall is indeed the easternmost point in the United States of America.

old plantation and full of beautiful Caribbean blooms. The greathouse has been renovated and now plays host to a variety of activities, from art exhibitions to weddings. There are a number of other buildings that were part of the St. George plantation, plus a number of garden areas. Among these are a small but beautiful orchid house, a cactus garden, and a re-creation of a bush medicine garden, where you can read about the purpose and preparation of each plant medication.

On your left a little farther along Route 70 is the **Cruzan Rum Distillery**. Rum is synonymous with the Caribbean, and Virgin Islands rum was so well regarded that George Washington supplied it to his troops at Valley Forge. Today, the distilling tradition is carried on under the trade name Cruzan Rum. Twenty-minute tours give you a comprehensive look around the surprisingly small plant and of course allow you to taste the end result and buy a few bottles to dispose of at your leisure. The plant uses only pure St. Croix rainwater in its rum. This is said to account for the clean taste and the supposed lack of hangover after drinking, but you should proceed with caution nonetheless.

A short distance away is **Estate Whim Plantation Museum**. The highlight of the tour of this Danish plantation is the greathouse, the best example of a Danish colonial residence in the Virgin Islands. Built in Neo-Classical style in the early 18th century, the house has a simple design with features that dissipated the heat in the days before air-conditioning. The furniture sits amid cool, pale blue and gray walls and the limed wooden floors so beloved of Danish designers today. Interestingly, the house was constructed with a mortar that contained molasses, an unusual use for one of the major products of the plantation. Surrounding the house are vestiges of the working plant, such as the mill and the cane press. The greathouse is used for regular recitals and other community activities.

Frederiksted

The second-largest settlement on St. Croix, **Frederiksted**, is on the western coastline at the end of Route 70. It is a sleepy town with hints of the grandeur that must have existed during

The Weed Women

The weed women were slaves who held positions of respect in plantation life. They were often the only medical practitioners for both the slave and colonial populations, with knowledge of how to use various plant species as medicines and how to find, pick, mix, and apply them in an effective way. Today's practitioners are known as bush doctors or (more commonly elsewhere) herbalists.

Bananas and other tropical delights can be found at the St. George Botanical Garden.

Danish rule. Many buildings remain permanently shuttered, hiding the treasures within. In 1878 a local uprising resulted in a fire that destroyed half of the old town. Tropical storms have continued the physical transformation to the present day.

Frederiksted might look like a ghost town, but when a cruise ship arrives, local businesses open their shutters and doors to welcome the visitors. Every other Wednesday, the cruise ship *Destiny* hits town and doesn't leave port until midnight. The whole town goes into party mode on what is called Harbor Night. Shops stay open, stilt walkers and street musicians perform, and everyone has a great time.

Fort Frederik guards the waterfront and the dock for the cruise ships. Completed in 1760, it was named after the Danish monarch in power at the time, Frederik V. The fort was small but played a crucial role in protecting the shipping lanes against privateers and providing a place of refuge for islanders in case of hurricane. It was also the first fort to fire a salute to the newly declared United States of America on 25 October 1776. In 1848 the emancipation of the slaves was declared from here by Governor-General Peter von Scholten. Fort Frederik later became a library, telephone exchange, and police station before renovations were completed in 1976. Today, it looks much as it would have in 1760 and houses a local history museum. Two of the old barracks have displays about hurricanes on the islands over the centuries, including a graphic video of the aftermath of Hurricane Hugo in 1989.

Southeast of Frederiksted is **Sandy Point**, one of the main turtle-breeding beaches on St. Croix. To return to Christiansted, head north out of town on Route 63 and take a left at Route 76 to enjoy a scenic journey.

As soon as you leave the coastal plain, the vegetation becomes much more lush and the air more humid. Huge ferns and other tropical plants hug the road, creating a tunnel of foliage. This is St. Croix's **Rain Forest**. Although technically it is only semitropical, it still provides sharp contrast to the more arid eastern portion of the island.

Once through the rain forest, turn north toward the coast. The long hill that you travel down is known locally as "the Beast," one of the most formidable stretches of the international triathlon that takes place on St. Croix each year. Runners actually travel in the other direction, going uphill rather than down. Once at the coast, take a right. This portion of the coastal route has sweeping views and wide curves that have figured in a number of movies as a substitute for California's Big Sur coastline.

Eventually the road leads to **Salt River Bay**, the place where European influence in the Virgin Islands began when Columbus set foot here in 1493. His less-than-friendly encounter with the Carib Indians caused him to name the place Cabo de Flechas ("Cape of the Arrows"). Today there is a national park protecting the site and the mangrove swamps of the river inlet. A small plaque laid in 1975 marks this spot's importance in Virgin Islands history.

All fired up at Fort Frederik — the first fort to fire a salute to the newly declared US on 25 October 1776.

THE BRITISH VIRGIN ISLANDS

The **British Virgin Islands** (BVI) lie beside the American islands, yet might be a world away. The pace moves much more slowly and the constant buzz of air-conditioning heard on the USVI is far less common here. You'll see small herds of goats grazing on the roadsides and somnolent cats resting in the shade. Conversation in bars and under the shade of trees centers on cricket and local gossip. Service is decidedly relaxed in shops and restaurants.

The BVI are one of the main destinations for the world's yachtsmen. The fact that there are dozens of islands with anchorages means that sailing is both safe and exciting. Most other activities also center on the water—diving, snorkeling, and just relaxing on the beach are the favorite tourist pursuits. For stress relief, the BVI will provide the kind of benefits for which you'd gladly pay a therapist thousands of dollars.

Virgin Islands Attractions

St. Thomas

Fort Christian. Open Monday–Friday 8:30am–4:30pm, Saturday 10am–3pm; Tel. (340) 776-4566.

St. Thomas Synagogue. Open Monday–Friday during daylight hours; Tel. (340) 774-4312.

Legislature Building. Sessions of the USVI Senate are open to the public; Tel. (340) 774-0880.

Estate St. Peter Greathouse and Botanical Gardens. Open daily 9am–4:30pm; Tel. (340) 774-4999.

Mountain Top. Views and banana daiquiris. Open daily.

Coral World. Open daily 9am–5pm; Tel. (340) 775-1555.

Paradise Point Tramway. Open daily 9am–9pm; Tel. (340) 774-9809.

St. John

Virgin Islands National Park Visitors' Center in Cruz Bay. Open daily 8am–4:30pm; Tel. (340) 776-6201.

St. Croix

Fort Christiansvaern and Scale House. Open daily 8am–5pm; Tel. (340) 773-1460.

Steeple Building. Open daily 9am–4:30pm; Tel. (340) 773-1460.

Estate Whim Plantation Museum. Open Monday–Saturday 10am–4pm; Tel. (340) 772-0598.

Fort Frederik. Open Monday–Friday 8:30am–4pm; Tel. (340) 772-2021.

St. Croix Aquarium and Marine Education Center. Open Tuesday–Saturday 11am–4pm; Tel. (340) 773-8995.

Tortola

J. R. O'Neal Botanic Gardens. Flower shows and special events. Open daily from dawn to dusk; Tel. (284) 494-4557.

Tortola

Named "Turtle Dove" by the Spanish, the sleepy isle of **Tortola** is the capital of the British Virgin Islands. Home to about 14,000 of the BVI's approximately 20,000 residents, it dwarfs its immediate neighbors. Although it has undergone many changes in recent years, it still retains a quiet Caribbean charm.

Tortola has become the yacht-charter capital of the world, with several large harbors along the west coast. Every week hundreds of sailboats set out to explore the waters and islands of the BVI. Increasingly they are visiting the USVI, too, for a little international *détente*.

The local government is developing Tortola as an offshore banking center. That the islands sit under a British flag denotes their political stability, and banking laws passed in the Virgin Islands further protect their integrity and confidentiality. Businesses have flocked from South America and Hong Kong to turn Tortola into a player in the offshore finance market.

Road Town

The action centers on **Road Town**, Tortola's capital, in the center of the island on the southern coast. It is growing rapidly, with bank buildings adding a corporate flavor to the traditional pastel-colored wooden shacks of the old town. A cruise dock services an increasing amount of traffic, and the surrounding marinas can seem to be larger than the land-based buildings.

Main Street is the old artery through the town. A number of interesting little shops can be found here, housed in picture-perfect Caribbean shacks kept neat and tidy by their proprietors. Jewelry, art, and handicrafts figure highly here, but don't expect the international designer brands of the USVI. Those who love to browse in casual comfort will have a thoroughly enjoyable afternoon.

Festive Caribbean color is the order of the day at these shops on Road Town's Main Street.

The **Virgin Islands Folk Museum**, also on Main Street, is housed in a traditional West Indian building. It has displays of artifacts from various periods, including the Taino Indian, plantation, and slavery eras. There are also pieces from the wreck of the RMS *Rhone*.

Traffic has been diverted on a new highway running parallel to Main Street, which links to a two-lane highway carrying traffic around the harbor. Cross this road to reach the commercial ferry dock, where you can take boats other British Virgin Islands as well as the USVI. The tourist information office is also here, so you can pick up a copy of *Welcome* magazine, the official guide to the BVI, which is packed with information.

North from the ferry dock and across the rather ugly parking lot, you will find a small, colorful craft market where you

Savoring the catch of the day at a harborside restaurant in Wickham's Cay, Road Town.

can buy island clothing, spices and sauces, and the ever-present T-shirt. The nearby harbor of Wickham's Cay has slips for thousands of yachts and motorboats. There's a casual, enjoyable atmosphere in the bars and restaurants scattered around the waterfront.

The **J. R. O'Neal Botanical Gardens**, on the corner of Station Avenue and Main Street, is a five-minute walk from the ferry dock. It's small and peaceful, with indigenous as well as exotic tropical plants. Lizards scamper away as you approach, and chickens scratch in the undergrowth. There are benches where you can sit and enjoy the view; all have been donated by local families or corporations. Across Main Street you'll find the sports-ground, where locals play rugby in winter and cricket in summer. The crowds are small but very vocal, and you'll always find someone to explain the rules for you.

Around Tortola

Traveling around the island from Road Town, it is easy to see all of Tortola's attractions in one day—many who have taken this same journey in the past liked what they saw and never left! The road system around the island is simple and the surfaces are in reasonable condition, but Tortola has some of the fastest drivers in the Virgin Islands. You should be on your guard.

On your way to the island's western end, first travel south out of town past Fort Burt, once a pirate castle and now a hotel. You'll continue past Sea Cow Bay and Nanny Cay, both used for local small-scale industry and fishing. To the north lies Sage Mountain, which at 1780 ft (543 m) is the highest point on the island. It is surrounded by Mount Sage National Park, protecting what little is left of Tortola's rain forest.

> In the BVI people dress informally, in shorts and T-shirts, at all times. But no bare feet in town, please!

Once past Nanny Cay, the road offers very clear views of St. John. Take the left turn to **Frenchman's Cay**, a tiny peninsula with a small but popular marina called **Soper's Hole**. A large yacht fleet sails from here, but many land-based visitors like to visit the restaurants and shops housed in modern buildings designed to preserve traditional themes. Pastel colors and verdant foliage abound.

The main road leads eventually to the island's **West End** and the ferry port, where boats leave for St. Thomas and St. John. It is not easy to make your way around Steel Point at the far western tip of Tortola. Instead, head back to Zion Hill Road (the first major road to the north) to travel up and over the hill to the north shore. Here you will find a series of sandy bays to rival those on the north shore of St. John, although the surrounding land here has been settled. The road rises high over the headlands to offer wonderful views of the beaches.

When you reach the North Coast Road, take a left turn to go west to **Long Bay**. The surfaced road finishes after the Long Bay Beach Resort, but persevere (unless your transport is totally inadequate) and follow the small wooden signs for **Smugglers Cove**, one of the best kept secrets on Tortola. It is only 5 minutes on the unpaved road, past Belmont Pond (now cut off from the sea), before you come upon a splendid arc of sand. Hunt out the Smugglers Cove Hotel, situated in the sea grapes that line the beach, for a few lessons in modern history. Owner Bob Dennison decided—after several storms—not to repair the old hotel and now runs a self-service honor bar on the remains of his property. He also loaned a 1966 Lincoln Continental to the Virgin Islands authorities when Queen Elizabeth visited the island in 1977. She traveled the island in the car, which takes pride of place in the shell of the storm-damaged hotel. Unfortunately, it needs a little body work, but Bob is waiting for the next royal visit before he makes the effort.

Retrace your steps through Long Bay and continue back east along the North Coast Road. You next reach **Apple Bay**, home of Bomba's Surfside Shack, which hosts the largest party on the island every full moon. The shack is little more than a few pieces of wood, every inch covered with graffiti and other items left by visitors. Stop by in the evening to sample the atmosphere.

Head past Little Carrot Bay and Great Carrot Bay, where the road will climb steeply up the hillside. Once over the ridge you will catch your first glimpse of **Cane Garden Bay**, arguably the best beach on Tortola. It is true that the sand is wonderful,

Secretive past...and secretive present. Smuggler's Cove is one of Tortola's best-kept secrets.

the seas clear and warm, and diving pelicans join you in snorkeling. But more than this, Cane Garden Bay is a burgeoning resort in its own right, with small European-style hotels and apartments and several restaurants. Many cruise-ship passengers make their way here once they dock, so check on ship times to avoid the crowds.

From Cane Garden Bay, the main road heads inland and up into the mountainous center of the island. On reaching Leonards, high in the interior, take the left turn onto Ridge Road, then left again to **Skyworld**. This small platform, along with its gift shop and restaurant (reservations required), offers spectacular views over the surrounding water and islands, particularly at sunset.

Ridge Road heads toward Tortola's **East End**. A left turn toward the water brings you to **Brewers Bay**, where

Working holiday: boaters flex biceps at Cane Garden Bay.

you'll find a campsite and great snorkeling. Mount Healthy National Park sits above the bay but is little more than the remains of an old windmill.

Eventually Ridge Road drops to **Long Look–East End**, an amalgamation of two settlements at the eastern tip of the island and the last destination before the road crosses the **Queen Elizabeth II Bridge**. This single-track iron bridge (plans for another lane are in the pipeline), opened by the Queen in 1977, takes you off Tortola. Once on the other side you are on tiny **Beef Island**, home to the main airport serving the BVI.

The airport is surprisingly busy, with small commercial turbo-prop planes from Puerto Rico and St. Thomas and light charter planes that fly to other islands — or anywhere you want them to go. Next to the airport is the sheltered harbor of **Trellis Bay**, with ferry service to Bitter End Yacht Club, Virgin Gorda. A couple of restaurants serve the sailors who drop anchor here.

Head back south and west along the coast toward Road Town, where you will be greeted by wonderful views over Sir Francis Drake Channel to a chain of other British islands. Ginger, Cooper, and Salt are the closest.

Virgin Gorda

When Columbus caught sight of this island, he christened it **Virgin Gorda** (the "Pregnant" or "Fat" Virgin) because of its very unusual shape. The outline resembles a reclining figure with distended stomach, so high are the hills of the interior. The land is split into two quite separate areas: the Valley or flat lowland to the west, where most of the population of 3,500 lives, and the mountains to the east, which form a barrier to settlement and communication. The lowland is characterized by massive boulders strewn across the land as if by a giant's hand. Almost everywhere there are signs of a dry climate. Several cactus species thrive here, and ground-hugging varieties vie with tall century plants for access to the precious water. Goats and chickens eke out a living from the parched soil, sauntering across the main roads.

Many of Virgin Gorda's visitors are yachtsmen and boaters. In fact, the best and easiest way to explore the island is by water. Some of the best beaches and coves and even certain resort hotels are accessible only by boat. But this doesn't mean that you miss out by taking to the road. You can enjoy many of the island's delights if you take a taxi ride or a tour.

Wild Goats

Many of the islands have populations of wild goats, particularly in the BVI, where they regularly impede road traffic and eat the flowers and vegetables carefully tended by householders. Goats are not indigenous to the Virgin Islands but were a source of food for the pirates who sailed the waters here. They put the goats ashore to graze, sailed off in search of booty, and then returned to catch a couple of goats to provide meat for their next journey. When the pirates were finally driven out of the islands, the goats carried on, happily eating and multiplying.

The island is quite small—about 8 miles (13 km) long and 2 miles (3 km) wide at most—and there are few attractions to visit. The biggest appeal for those who return here year after year is the chance simply to relax and do nothing. So after a day of touring, settle down with a cool drink and watch the yachtsmen do all the hard work.

Spanish Town

The capital of Virgin Gorda is **Spanish Town**, which is in reality barely a town. It sprawls outward from the tiny commercial port, with houses and small stores interspersed among the rocks. For visitors, the main attraction is the **Virgin Gorda Yacht Club**, a large marina 200 yards (183 m) to the west of the docks. You'll find the tourist information office here, along with a bank, shops, restaurants, and bars. If you want to arrange sailing, fishing, day cruises, or jet skiing, a number of companies operate out of the Yacht Club harbor, and taxis wait to whisk people off to see the sights.

Around Virgin Gorda

From Spanish Town, most people head straight for Virgin Gorda's most famous attraction, the **Baths**. These are situated a quick taxi ride to the south. The Baths is a 1-mile (1½-km) stretch of coastline where thousands of huge boulders lie strewn along the water's edge. Rocks worn smooth by waves and wind nestle together to create caves and caverns. Walkways between the boulders beckon the adventurous, who find shaded, cool sand interspersed with exquisite sunny beaches. The shapes and shadows are almost surreal and change constantly as the sun moves across the

Tiny Beef Island is home to the BVI's main airport, and to secluded Trellis Bay pictured here.

sky, striking shafts of light into their midst. Out in the crystal clear water there is a snorkeler's paradise, while a collection of yachts bob offshore, their passengers diving from the decks to enjoy a cool swim.

If you come here by road, you will arrive at the top of the hill, where there are a few restaurants. It is then a 600-yard (659-m) downhill walk to reach the Baths. Getting to the first beach is easy, but following the trail to **Devil's Bay** requires some fitness. Slippery, sand-covered rocks and narrow, low tunnels mean a lot of bending, crouching, and climbing in order to get to the most spectacular sections. Incidentally, a walking trail to the west of the main footpath leads you to the most westerly

bays without having to climb through the boulders. This would be a better option for small children or the elderly.

Just off the west coast of Virgin Gorda is a small island called **Fallen Jerusalem**. It is covered with boulders similar to those at the Baths and resembles a ruined ancient city. Head back in the direction of Spanish Town for a fascinating historical attraction, perhaps the only one on Virgin Gorda. Turn right at Long Road and right again at Rhymer Road, then continue

A colorful shop advertisement beckons the passersby in Virgin Gorda.

even after the pavement gives way to a dirt road (the route is not difficult). If you pass the Mineshaft Café and Pub, you are on the right path. The road leads along the east coast, where the waves of the Atlantic Ocean pound the shoreline.

At the very end of the road are the remains of the **Copper Mine**, worked between the years of 1837 and 1862 and unique in the eastern Caribbean. In 1837, 36 tin miners arrived from Cornwall in England to work a supposedly rich source of copper. These hardy men were joined by 140 Virgin Islanders and sank the first shaft in 1838. At their deepest, the shafts reach 240 ft (73 m) below ground. Unfortunately, within a generation the mine was spent and the buildings were left to the elements. Now they sit as a lonely memorial to the miners, the stack and engine house clearly visible. Although there are many green rocks containing copper ore, the site has been designated as historically important, and no stones may be removed for souvenirs.

If you want to wait before attempting the spectacular ride up and over the mountains, stop a while at **Little Dix Bay**, just on the eastern outskirts of Spanish Town. The beach here is beautiful and sheltered, serving the guests of Little Dix Bay Resort—sister resort to Caneel Bay on St. John and built by Laurance Rockefeller. The thatched umbrellas lining the beach add an extra dimension to the tropical allure here, especially for photographs. However, these are for hotel guests only; bring your own towels and umbrellas if you want to swim or sunbathe. The resort puts on an excellent buffet lunch, which is open to non-guests, so it's a good spot for a break in the itinerary, if only to get a glimpse of the lovely manicured grounds.

Only one road leads across the heart of the island toward North Sound, where a cluster of settlements has developed in recent years. North Sound Road runs like a backbone along the side of the central hills. The ride is extremely exhilarating and offers wonderful views back over the valley. On a clear day you can see down the full length of Sir Francis Drake Channel and its islands, all the way to St. John.

Just before the big climb begins, you will be able to stop and admire the long fringe of sand at **Savannah Bay**. The waters are excellent for snorkeling, with areas of shallow rock and reef only yards from the shore. Watch out for a sign to **Nail Bay** off to the left. This developing area along Virgin Gorda's northeast coast is served by a poor but improving road.

After Savannah Bay, the road begins to climb steeply. Within a couple of minutes you rise nearly a thousand feet into the **Virgin Gorda Peak National Park**. Two small signs identify trails leading to the summit at 1,359 ft (414 m). The first is a 45-minute walk through the vegetation; the second begins much closer to the summit. Your choice depends on your fitness and energy levels.

The main road continues; after the national park signs, you will catch the first views of **North Sound** and the northern tip of the island. The scene is truly spectacular as you

look down on one of the greatest anchorages in the Caribbean. On a busy day hundreds of sailboats and a dozen small cruise ships weigh anchor here to enjoy the beaches and resort facilities. Your taxi driver will know all the best places to stop for photographs, and you are sure to want to take a few.

The road drops toward North Sound as quickly as it rose. Those not wanting to take a ferry across the Sound should take the left fork for **Leverick Bay** (you'll see the sign), where

Devil's Bay, along Virgin Gorda's stunning, boulder-strewn coastline, the Baths.

there is a small but lively marina, rental condos, and houses. Shops and laundry facilities serve condo dwellers and yachtsmen alike, and one busy bar/restaurant provides the social focus. From here you can see **Mosquito Island** less

Best Beaches

UNITED STATES VIRGIN ISLANDS

Magen's Bay, St. Thomas. Wonderful fine sand and protected sea, with no tidal swell.

Coki Point, St. Thomas. Small sand beach benefiting from the Coral World facility. Here fish are fed regularly, which means excellent snorkeling; the fish swim all around the point, not just in the feeding area.

North shore of St. John. Perhaps the finest string of beaches anywhere in the world. From Hawksnest Bay to Francis Bay, each has fine sand and wonderful blue water.

Buck Island Reef National Monument, St. Croix. Protected waters mean wonderful and prolific sea life.

BRITISH VIRGIN ISLANDS

Smuggler's Cove, Tortola. Pristine, sandy curve with few other people. Enjoy it while you can.

Cane Garden Bay, Tortola. A true island beach where fishermen and fishing birds share the bay with sunbathers and watersports enthusiasts.

The Baths, Virgin Gorda. Unique rock formations create beauty and wonderful sandy coves.

Little Dix Bay, Virgin Gorda. This archetypal Caribbean beach has an arc of fine sand with a fine resort hotel—the best of all worlds.

White Bay, Jost Van Dyke. Truly wonderful sand and aqua waters. The Soggy Dollar bar is a bonus.

Anegada. An island surrounded by one long, fine white sand beach. Few facilities but perfect for those who want to get away from it all.

than half a mile (about 1 km) offshore, home to a quiet ex-clusive resort that will ferry non-guests from Leverick Bay for dinner at the hotel.

Those who want to see the resorts of North Sound must take the right fork to **Gun Creek**, where the road comes to a dead end. Any further progress must be by boat, but there is no public commercial ferry service. If you don't rent a boat, you'll need to contact the hotels for transport. For example, the Bitter End resort has a special "day member" policy. Even if you are not staying at the hotel, you can enjoy the re-sort and all its facilities for a fee. The resort is nearly the size of a small town and is a focal point for the yachting commu-nity, being home to the Bitter End Yacht Club. It hosts a number of activities throughout the year, and its New Year parties are second in size only to the ones on Jost Van Dyke. There is yachting, windsurfing, kayaking, and surfboarding (to name just a few of the amenities), all with instruction.

From Bitter End, it is just a short boat ride out to three pic-turesque islands. **Prickly Pear Island** has a wide expanse of beach that tends to get filled with "yachties" wanting to es-cape the boat for the day. It also has a great beach bar. Eusta-tia Island offers anchorages for wonderful snorkeling but is a private refuge. Its neighbor, Necker Island, is also private — perhaps the ultimate secluded getaway in the Virgin Islands.

Jost Van Dyke

This British island, lying northwest of Tortola and directly north of St. John, is thought to be named after a Dutch pi-rate. Its smaller brother, Little Jost Van Dyke, sits on its eastern flank. **Jost Van Dyke** (*Jost* is pronounced "Yost") has no towns to speak of, with a population of only a couple of hundred people, yet it is one of the most popular lunch spots in the Caribbean. You have to sail to get here, and

If this is the Bitter End, then life on the Virgin Islands must truly be paradise beyond all proportion!

private, charter, and day boats from both Tortola and the US islands (St. Thomas and St. John) jostle for the best spots on the two sandy beaches—which also have two of the most enjoyable bars in the Virgin Islands. There's nothing to do here but enjoy the sun and the amazingly translucent, aquamarine water.

Day boats will drop passengers at the jetty in **Great Harbor**, where a small customs station processes your paperwork and puts a stamp in your passport (you'll also need to pay a customs fee) if you travel from the USVI. Many people take the two-minute barefoot stroll along the seafront before settling down to lunch. Foxy's is probably the most famous restaurant here, where the owner's improvised Calypso songs are a constant accompaniment to the rum punch and island food. After lunch, many visitors move to **White Bay** for swimming, sunbathing, and a drink or two at the Soggy Dollar Bar, called this because, as there is no jetty here, most people have to get themselves and their money wet in order to reach the bar. For non-swimmers and those who simply want to stay dry, most day boats will provide a motorized tender to the shore and back.

Anegada

Anegada is unique in the Virgin Islands chain because it is the only coral formation among many hundreds of volcanic peaks. Its 33 sq miles (85 sq km) appear to be completely flat, and *Anegada* in fact means "sunken land." But local people boast that there are areas of land that rise to 28 ft (8½ m) above sea level. If only for its uniqueness, the island would be worth a look. Add to this, however, a ring of beaches with white sand as fine as talcum powder, clear blue waters for diving and snorkeling, and some fine bonefishing right from your doorstep (bonefish are known as the hardest species in the world to

> Many Virgin Islanders address each other with "Mr.," Mrs.," or "Miss" plus the surname—which makes for a pleasant level of formality.

catch), and Anegada becomes a special destination.

A shipwreck for every day of the year testifies to the danger of the reef surrounding the island. With just one entrance to the inner lagoon, only the most experienced captains attempt to bring a boat in here. And with little accommodation (only a few rooms and camping spots), you have the island totally to yourself—along with the 200 lucky people who get to call this place home.

There are no towns on Anegada. Most of the population lives in a loose collection of buildings called the Settle-

Away from it all...steal a spot for yourself and savor the silence. Here, in Anegada.

ment, on the southeast coast just beside the surprisingly good airstrip. A road of sorts (hard coral base covered in sand) encircles the island, running between the beaches and the salt lakes that cover a large proportion of the interior. Here you'll find a flock of wild flamingos adding grace and beauty to the brown, brackish water.

If you take time to travel around the island, you will find the handful of restaurants and small boat docks, or you can simply pick your own stretch of sublime beach where it seems there is nobody else in the world. If, instead, you decide you want company, **Loblolly Bay** (on the northeast coastline) is the place where everyone meets for snorkeling and a good lobster dinner. Those seeking a bit of culture should look in on Pomato Point Bar, Restaurant, and Museum at **Pomato Point** on the south coast. The contents—an eclectic collection of bottles, buttons, and pottery from shipwrecks around the island—won't give the Smithsonian or the Victoria and Albert a run for their money. But the setting and the museum's simplicity are totally in keeping with this most "desert island" of the Virgin Islands.

Other British Virgin Islands

A series of small islands lie to the south of Tortola, across the narrow stretch of sea called **Sir Francis Drake Channel**. Some are uninhabited and others are private domains. Yet all have fascinating stories to share, and some even have a few secrets yet to be revealed. Today they form a string of delightful yachting harbors and exciting diving and snorkeling sites. A few are the perfect "get-away-from-it-all" resorts.

The most southerly of these is **Norman Island**, situated close to the eastern tip of St. John in the USVI, which was named after a pirate named Norman — a rather nondescript moniker compared to "Blackbeard" or "Calico Jack." It is rumored that Norman buried a large cache of treasure somewhere on this island, but nobody has discovered its hiding place yet. Norman Island is said to have inspired Robert Louis Stevenson when he wrote *Treasure Island.*

Next is **Peter Island**, home to a deluxe resort with transfer boats from Road Town in Tortola. Many come to enjoy the snorkeling at Deadman's Bay and White Bay. Northeast of Peter Island is **Dead Chest**, which is really no more than a rock sticking out of the ocean. It is said to be the place where the pirate Blackbeard abandoned 15 of his bloodthirsty and mutinous crew, leaving them with only a bottle of rum and a cutlass. Probably the inspiration for the pirate anthem "15 men on a dead man's chest — Yo ho ho and a bottle of rum". Blackbeard returned later to find all of the men dead.

Salt Island was once a very important producer of this precious mineral. Its population made a decent living by harvesting and selling the salt to passing ships, where it was used to preserve meat for the long sea journeys and to trade for other goods. Although the business has long since lost its importance and the population has dwindled, Salt Island still has salt for sale and still sends the English monarch one sack of salt annually, just as it has done for generations. **Cooper Island** and **Ginger Island** lie east of Salt Island and begin the curve of islets north toward Virgin Gorda.

Between Salt and Peter islands lies a fascinating dive site. The wreck of HMS *Rhone,* a Royal Mail steamer that hit rocks and sank in 1867, lies in around 80 ft (24 m) of water and has become such a haven for fish and other marine life that it has been designated a marine park. The dive allows you to explore the interior of the ship as well as the site of the boiler explosion that caused her ultimate demise. The cold water entering through a tear in her side hit the hot boiler, and the resulting explosion broke up the ship.

Peter Island pampering: Ritzy accommodation is the name of the game at this deluxe resort.

WHAT TO DO

There is no shortage of things to do around the Virgin Islands, from shopping to sailing to dancing your evenings away. You'll find that each island is different in its particular style and in the amount and range of activities. Generally, the British Virgin Islands are quieter and more subdued, with fewer organized activities; the US Virgin Islands offer more variety and a greater range. But the best part of traveling to these tiny outposts is that you can have it all: by taking a short boat trip from your "home" island to a neighboring island, you can savor its particular amenities for a few hours or an entire day.

INTER-ISLAND EXCURSIONS

Just because you decide to stay on one Virgin Island doesn't mean that you can't see a number of others during your stay. Because the US and British Virgin Islands are so close, it is simple to cross borders and shop in Charlotte Amalie if you are staying on Tortola, or to visit the world famous Baths on Virgin Gorda if you are staying on St. Thomas or St. John.

Regular ferry services make island-hopping surprisingly easy and relatively cheap. Commercial flights also offer a quick and exciting way to see other islands.

Within the USVI

It is simple to visit any of the other main islands from your vacation base. The link between St. Thomas and St. John is the easiest, with 19 services daily between Red Hook on the east coast of St. Thomas and Cruz Bay. This service does not stop until midnight, so it is quite feasible to stay in St. Thomas and have a day on the beach at St. John, stay for dinner in Cruz Bay, and still be back at your base hotel in time for a nightcap.

Contact Transportation Services (tel: 340/776-6282). There is also a car ferry from Red Hook to Cruz Bay; contact Boyson Inc. (tel: 340/776-6294) or Republic Barge (tel: 340/779-4000). The ferry service from Charlotte Amalie to Cruz Bay runs 6 times per day (Contact Transportation Services).

Between St. Croix and the other islands, services are more limited. But it is possible to have a trip to quiet Christiansted if you stay in busy St. Thomas or unspoiled St. John. Hydrofoil Services (tel: 340/776-7417) operates from Charlotte Amalie to Christiansted. Seaborne Aviation operates seaplane services from the waterfront at Charlotte Amalie and offers pleasure flights around the US and British Virgin Islands or scheduled services from downtown Charlotte Amalie to downtown Christiansted several times daily (tel: 340/777-4491, or 888-FLY-TOUR toll-free in the US).

Within the BVI

For island-hopping around the BVI, chartering your own boat to use as a "hotel" is the ideal scenario. However, for those who prefer land-based accommodations, Tortola is the hub for a number of scheduled ferry services to other British islands, including Jost Van Dyke, Virgin Gorda, Norman Island, and Peter Island. Many private day charters will take you to more out-of-the-way islands if the demand is high enough.

All commercial ferries depart from the same small dock on the west side of the harbor in Road Town. Speedy's Ferry Service offers a special day-trip from Tortola to Virgin Gorda, including taxi service to the Baths plus lunch, or a regular service four times daily (tel: 284/495-5240). Smith's Ferry operates a competing service at slightly different times (tel: 284/495-4495), as does Native Son (tel: 284/495-4617). A ferry runs four times daily, Monday through Saturday, from West End Tortola to Jost Van Dyke, and three times on

Island-hopping in a matter of minutes…An inter-island sea plane prepares for take-off, St. Thomas.

Sunday (tel: 284/494-2997). There is also a ferry from Road Town to Peter Island eight times daily (tel: 284/495-2000).

From Tortola, take a flight to Anegada and rent a car to enjoy a day on a desert island. Clair Aero offers regular services from Beef Island airport, allowing you to spend several hours on Anegada (tel: 284/495-2271).

Between the USVI and the BVI

There are numerous commercial ferry services linking the USVI and the BVI. Provided that you have proof of citizenship, the formalities involved in crossing the borders are simple and straightforward.

Smith's Ferries (tel: 340/775-7292) and Native Son Inc. (tel: 340/774-8685) both go to Tortola from the Marine

On the waterfront, it's never dull at busy Soper's Hole marina, on Tortola's West End.

Terminal on the Charlotte Amalie waterfront. You can then catch connecting ferries to Virgin Gorda (see above). Interisland (tel: 340/776-6597) offers a ferry service linking Cruz Bay (St. John), Red Hook (St. Thomas), West End (Tortola), and Jost Van Dyke.

Smith's Ferries also operates a Saturday-only service from Charlotte Amalie to Virgin Gorda and Tortola. Limnos Charters offers stops for swimming at the Baths on Virgin Gorda and snorkeling at the Caves of Norman Island; they operate from bases at St. John and St. Thomas (tel: 340/775-3203).

For air travel, Seaborne Aviation (see page 82) has a service to West End in Tortola from Charlotte Amalie (just an eight-minute flight). Air Sunshine operates daily flights from St. Croix to Beef Island Airport on Tortola (tel: 284/495-8900).

SHOPPING

In the USVI

The US Virgin Islands are famous for their shopping opportunities. Their legacy of Danish rule and their pivotal role as a trading nation in the Caribbean set the scene for today's shopping centers. The tax-free status of St. Thomas, St. John, and St. Croix means bargains galore, combined with generous duty-free allowances for American citizens who shop here. Even for non-residents of the US, the Virgin Islands still offer a wealth of shopping possibilities. The relaxation of duty

Whether you're treating yourself or shopping for gifts, the USVI's tax-free status makes it easy on the budget.

Artist at work: a folk art craftsman adds finishing touches, Charlotte Amalie.

rules for Americans has attracted some of the finest names in designer goods and a wide range of merchandise.

St. Thomas is obviously the big player as far as shopping is concerned. Charlotte Amalie has long been a popular trading port, and the opportunities here, in the narrow alleys of the Royal Dane Mall and Drake's Passage, or along the streets parallel to the waterfront, are probably some of the best in the world. The two other US islands offer interesting opportunities but are not as comprehensive as the treasure trove that is downtown Charlotte Amalie.

Jewelry and gems figure highly throughout the US Virgin Islands. You can buy gold by weight for necklaces or bracelets, loose gemstones in all cuts and sizes, or stones in the most elaborate settings. Watches by all the finest manufacturers are available here, and you can buy a watch for diving or one made of solid gold.

For jewelry produced on the islands, look for sand dollar, dolphin, and turtle designs in gold and silver. St. Croix has its own unique design: the hook bracelet that is a modern gold-and-silver replica of the traditional courtship bracelet.

For those who want to take something unique home from the islands, the USVI don't disappoint. The natural beauty here has always attracted artists, sculptors, and potters along with native craftspeople. You will find pottery, ceramics, costume jewelry, and island clothing, all in great variety.

Duty-free liquor is also available, with famous brand names from around the world. Bourbon, rum, cognac, and hundreds of flavored drinks line the walls of shops housed in the old Danish warehouses that sold the same goods over 200 years ago. Don't forget to take home a bottle of Cruzan rum.

As with any supposed bargain prices (savings of up to 40 percent are often advertised), it pays to do some research about prices and brands before you leave home. You can then be confident that you have really cut a good deal and not been taken for "tourist" prices.

In the BVI

There are far fewer shopping opportunities in the British islands than in the USVI. The BVI are not the place to come with a shopping list of goodies you want to take home. It is more a matter of browsing in the small souvenir or craft shops, many housed in quaint pastel-

Enticing Caribbean spices for food lovers at the Road Town market.

It's not just the garments—Road Town's stalls also come in a rainbow of colors.

painted Caribbean shacks. Art and craft work is the standout here, with locally produced jewelry being one of the nicest things to take home. You can pick up a sarong for the beach or a T-shirt, perhaps even a bottle or two of Pusser's Rum (once a regular drink of Her Majesty's Royal Navy).

Island spices, seasonings, and chutneys are also found in great abundance. The bottles and jars come topped with little straw hats or bandannas, and the contents are all delicious. Do be careful with the hot sauces—a little goes a long way.

BEACHES AND WATER SPORTS

Beaches abound on the Virgin Islands, and many visitors rate these as the top attraction. St. John has perhaps the most famous string of beaches on its northern shore. Without doubt they are breathtaking, and a few places here are still secluded.

However, all the Virgin Islands have beautiful beaches (see page 74), and each island also has resorts and hotels that offer comprehensive water sports facilities. Jet skiing, parasailing, kayaking, and sailing can be enjoyed at all the major resorts.

Diving

The Virgin Islands offer pristine waters and a wealth of natural reefs and artificial dive sites to explore. Divers have a chance to see turtles, sharks, and barracuda in their natural environment, and the warm waters mean that diving is exciting and comfortable throughout the year.

All the Virgin Islands have opportunities for certified divers. In the USVI, two of the most exciting dive sites are **Buck Island Reef National Monument**, which offers interesting diving in wonderfully clear waters, and **Thatch Cay**, a site full of sealife, with natural arches and tunnels.

There are equally compelling locations to dive in the BVI. The HMS *Rhone* was a mail steamer that in 1867 exploded and broke in two just west of Salt Island and south of Tortola. Divers can swim inside the hull, which is now home to hundreds of fish. **The Indians** are a cave system off Norman

Preparing for the plunge: Scuba divers off Cruz Bay, St. John.

Sea creatures: much of the Virgin Islands' best sightseeing is underwater, so grab a snorkel and jump in!

Island where divers and snorkelers can enjoy calm, protected waters. And **Blond Rock**, a more remote site off Peter Island, boasts dramatic ledges where there is the chance to see larger fish species along with sharks and turtles.

Remember to bring your dive certificate, as you will be allowed to rent equipment and dive only if you can prove your competence. If you wish to learn to dive in the Virgin Islands, there is an excellent network of dive centers providing training to professional levels. All centers are affiliated with one of the major certifying bodies, with PADI (Professional

Association of Diving Instructors) being the most common. There are a number of reputable companies in the islands offering diving training and instruction, among them:

St. Thomas: Chris Sawyer Diving Center operates out of the Renaissance Grand Resort; tel: 340/775-7804.

St. John: Operators out of Cruz Bay (such as Cruz Bay Watersports; tel: 340/776-6234) take divers out along the reefs of the north coast and shallow areas between the island and St. Thomas.

St. Croix: Mile Mark Watersports offers instruction and rental; 59 King's Wharf, Christiansted; tel: 340/773-2628.

Tortola: Baskin-in-the-Sun at Soper's Hole and Prospect Reef Hotel Marina; tel: 284/494 2858.

Virgin Gorda: Dive BVI has centers at Virgin Gorda Yacht Harbor (tel: 284/495-5513) and Leverick Bay (tel: 284/495-7328) and serves all the major hotels on Virgin Gorda.

Snorkeling

The Virgin Islands have some of the most beautiful snorkeling sites in the world. They also feature a number of places where novice snorkelers can see a wide variety of both fish and coral life under the watchful eyes of lifeguards, and marked trails where information plaques identify the species of fauna and fish. Most companies operating dive boats will also organize snorkel trips to sheltered bays or offshore sites, and many day charters or sails provide some time in the schedule for snorkeling.

Good snorkeling areas scattered through the Virgin Islands include Coki Point on St. Thomas, Trunk Bay on St. John, Buck Island off St. Croix, Brewer's Bay on Tortola, the Baths at Virgin Gorda, and the Caves off Norman Island. But in the Virgin Islands it is possible to swim in the water almost anywhere and enjoy the marine life.

Calendar of Events

(see page 121 for public holidays throughout the islands)

March. Virgin Gorda Festival culminates on Easter Sunday.

31 March. Celebration of the official transfer of the Danish West Indian Islands to the United States.

April. St. Croix International Triathlon; St. Thomas Carnival (follows Easter); BVI Spring Regatta.

4 July. Culmination of the St. John Carnival.

14 July. Bastille Day (Frenchtown, Charlotte Amalie).

August. The USVI Open Atlantic Blue Marlin Tournament; BVI Sportfishing Tournament; BVI Summer Festival.

September. BVI International Rugby Festival (Tortola); Foxy's Wooden Boat Regatta (Jost Van Dyke).

November. St. Thomas/St. John Agricultural Fair; Thanksgiving Regatta; BVI Boat Show; Bitter End Invitational Regatta.

December. Carnival in St. Croix (from Christmas through 6 January).

31 December. New Year's Eve parties at Foxy's on Jost Van Dyke and at the Bitter End Yacht Club.

If you want to experience the thrill of diving or snorkeling but don't have the skills or the confidence, you can rent "snuba" equipment for a combination of scuba and snorkeling. Swim underwater watching the sea life while breathing from a tube that reaches up to the surface so that there is a constant supply of air. No training or qualifications are required, and it is a safe way to enjoy the underwater world (Virgin Islands Snuba Excursions, with locations on St. John and St. Thomas; tel: 340/693-8063).

Sailing

Renting a boat here is as easy as renting a car in other destinations. Boats vary from small runabouts, which will be sufficient to get you around the harbor and the coastal shallows, to large sailing yachts and motor launches for inter-island expeditions. Rental fees vary enormously.

The BVI have by far the most boats for charter, with Road Town in Tortola being one of the largest centers for boat charters in the world. A number of companies will rent boats with crew, or without — known as bare boats. You must have the appropriate certification to pilot the boat yourself. Moorings is one of the largest and most reputable companies, with offices at Moorings Mariner Inn, Tortola (tel: 284/494-2332; also in Clearwater FL at tel: 800-535-7289 toll-free in the US; website: www.moorings.com).

Companies on every island offer morning, day, or sunset cruises with crews; they'll have you back at the hotel in time for dinner. From Cruz Bay, St. John, Adventurer operates day trips to Jost Van Dyke as well as half- and full-day snorkel trips (tel: 340/693-8000, ext. 1832, or 340/693-7328), or you can sail and snorkel with Captain Phil on *Wayward Sailor* (tel: 340/693-8555; 340/776-6922). For day sailing in the waters around St. Croix and trips to Buck Island, try Mile Mark

Barracuda dreaming…The deep-water channels are teeming with fish, which makes sport fishing a popular activity.

Watersports (tel: 340/773-2628). Contact companies such as Dive BVI for day-trips to Anegada from Virgin Gorda (tel: 284/495-7328 and 284/495-5513).

Sport and Deep-Sea Fishing

The warm seas around the islands are teeming with fish, and the deep-water channels (between St. Thomas and St. John, for example) offer passage to such species as barracuda, marlin, sailfish, tuna, and shark. Although conservation rules are strictly enforced, both sport fishing and line fishing can be great fun and extremely profitable. Sport fishing (that is, catching a fish to throw it back rather than to eat) is hugely popular, and fishing for large fish from powerful boats can be arranged on just about every island. The local guides are experienced and helpful. Bonefishing is big business, especially on the flats around Anegada, where you can catch these creatures from within feet of the shore. Bonefish are large, strong, inedible fish that frequent the shallows and sand flats. They are said to be the most difficult species in the world to catch.

Sport fishing boats can be rented at most major marinas in the USVI and BVI. The *Marlin Prince* operates out of Red Hook, St. Thomas (tel: 340/693-5929), Pelican Charters operates at the Prospect Reef Hotel marina in Road Town, Tortola (tel: 284/496-7386) and Grand Slam Fishing is also in Road Town (tel: 284/494-1535; 284/499-8420).

RECREATION ON LAND

Golf

Although not as well known for golf as perhaps Bermuda or Jamaica, the Virgin Islands do offer opportunities for those who can't go a week without playing a round. On St. Thomas, the Mahogany Run course is famed for its "devil's triangle," a trio of holes with very difficult approaches across

---

Warning: This Is NOT a Fruit!!

The innocuous-looking *manchineel* tree has small fruit resembling apples and leaves resembling a ficus plant. However, it is extremely hazardous. The fruit is poisonous (Columbus lost several of his crew after they ate it), and the bark can cause skin rashes. When it rains, the effect of the water running off the caustic leaves and branches can leave you with burns. Wash your hands after touching it and do not rub your eyes, as this can cause severe swelling.

the water to greens on the opposite hillside. The course occupies a stunning site backing onto Magen's Bay beach and has a comfortable clubhouse for socializing.

St. Croix has two 18-hole courses. One is at the Buccaneer Resort, to the east of Christiansted. The other is Carambola in the west of the island, a par-72 course designed by Robert Trent Jones and used by the Ladies' PGA for competitions. The Reef at Teague Bay has a nine-hole course.

Hiking

The great outdoors attract many visitors to the Virgin islands. Most enjoy sitting on the beach or sailing, but a few hardy souls make use of the trails that traverse some of the islands, for hikes through the natural vegetation. The center of this activity is the United States Virgin Islands National Park on St. John. The national park preserves vast expanses of forest, with 22 nature trails of varying lengths. The most popular lead from Cinnamon Bay out into the surrounding hills; another popular trail takes in the petroglyph rocks on the south side of the island. The Annaberg Sugar Plantation Ruins Walk is quite short but wonderfully scenic. The park office in Cruz Bay has maps and information.

The hiking in the BVI is not as organized, but there are trails on two islands. Virgin Gorda has trails through Gorda National Park (around Gorda Peak) and in the area around the Baths. Jost Van Dyke also has exciting trails into its interior.

ENTERTAINMENT

The Virgin Islands are not all beaches and sunshine. Locally, there is an abundant variety of Caribbean music heard in

Who can focus on the green with all that blue? St. Thomas's Mahogany Run golf course, as gorgeous as it is challenging.

nightclubs and bars, for dancing or just listening. Calypso, reggae, salsa, scratch bands (with guitars, saxophone, and drums, plus homemade instruments from gourds), and steel pan bands (often called steel "drums") vie for your attention with the more ubiquitous rock and jazz. It might be harder to find examples of the Virgin Islands' traditional dance, known as the quadrille; each island will have its own style.

The British islands are generally rather quiet. Many in the sailing community like to sit near the waterfront in bars and tell tall stories. For most sailors, dinner and a drink are usually followed by bedtime. There are a number of exceptions. Bomba's Surfside Shack (in Apple Bay, on the north coast of Tortola) holds a wild party each full moon and is swinging on weekend evenings. Many other bars have live music. The best known is Foxy's Tamarind Bar on Jost Van Dyke where you can hear the legendary calypsonian Foxy. All the islands come to life in late July and early August, when the BVI hold an annual week-long festival of parades, music, horse races, arts, and crafts. To get all the latest information, check the magazine *Welcome,* which you can pick up at tourist offices, as well as the weekly *Limin' Times.*

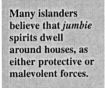

Many islanders believe that *jumbie* spirits dwell around houses, as either protective or malevolent forces.

On the USVI, things are a little different. Where there is a large local population and many more visitors, the cultural events and nightlife are a little more energetic. For lovers of the performing arts, the Reichhold Center for the Arts on St. Thomas (on the campus of the University of the Virgin Islands) has an annual series of concerts and dance events. On St. Croix, there is the Caribbean Dance Company, founded in 1977, as well as concerts and Broadway musicals at the Island Center (north of Sunny Isle).

Calypso tunes à la "Foxy!" The owner of Foxy's Bar, this performer is something of a celebrity on Jost Van Dyke.

St. Croix has perhaps the greatest range of after-dark activities in the Virgin Islands. Its casino facility at Carina Bay supplements the nightclubs and bars in Christiansted. *St. Croix This Week* will give you tips on all sorts of entertainment.

On St. Thomas, Charlotte Amalie has a number of music bars that stay open into the small hours, and many of the large resort hotels offer Caribbean shows or other entertainment, plus live piano music. Check out *St. Thomas This Week* (including St. John) for the latest information.

Throughout the islands, the Caribbean tradition of carnival and other colorful parades is carried on with gusto; each island will celebrate its own carnival at a different time of year. Street parades, calypso, scratch bands, steel pan bands, and the "mocko jumbie" (a West African spirit figure carried on stilts) add to the atmosphere. Just be sure to bring your widest smile and enjoy the day.

ACTIVITIES FOR CHILDREN

There's nothing that young visitors like better than a sandy beach and the sea, where they can play for hours in the shallow waters or build sandcastles. The Virgin Islands have some of the best public beaches in the world, most of which have facilities for refreshment and restrooms. Magen's Bay on St. Thomas, along with the north shore beaches of St. John, are ideal for children. For older children, the beach can still hold

The Coral World shark exhibit will enthrall kids and adults alike.

a fascination. Snorkeling and nonmotorized watersports can fill the whole day.

Always remember to cover young skin with a suitable sun-protection product and to limit their time in the sun for the first few days. Also make sure that they are well supervised whenever they are near the water.

Most large hotels will offer special activities for children. Always research the facilities available at any hotel before you make a reservation.

Here are some attractions that are ideal for younger visitors:

Coral World (St. Thomas). Pet a shark and watch the feeding sessions for numerous marine animals and fish.

Atlantis submarine (St. Thomas). Travel underwater in safety to spot fish, rays, and sharks as well as shipwrecks.

Day sails (all islands). With the proper safety equipment, kids can get out on the ocean waves.

Iguana spotting. These large but harmless lizards are all over the main islands.

The forts (Charlotte Amalie and St. Croix). Explore the history of the islands and have fun at the same time.

Mermaids on the rocks: sheltered Trellis Bay is a perfect kid-friendly beach.

EATING OUT

With the wide availability of international cuisine combined with interesting and tasty local dishes, there should always be something on the menu to please everyone. However, you will still find differences as you travel between islands and across the border between the BVI and USVI.

The close ties that the British islands still have with other British and former British societies throughout the Caribbean chain (including Barbados, Trinidad, and Jamaica) have kept the traditions of West Indian cooking alive much more than in the US islands. St. Croix still has a Danish influence and a surprising number of fine European-style restaurants.

What to Eat

If you leave the standard hotel fare behind, eating can be an exciting adventure. It's quite astonishing what local cooks do with island vegetables and fruits. Indeed, islanders can turn the humble coconut into coconut soup, coconut-and-avocado salad, frozen coconut chips, coconut-corn bread, coconut dumplings, coconut-cheese tart, coconut ice cream, and coconut daiquiris.

Conch fritters could well be on the menu, as might chilled papaya with fresh lime juice. Deep-fried banana or plantain chips and fritters are concepts imported by the sizable Puerto Rican community, as is *escaheche* (pickled fish served cold). Everybody makes avocado purées.

While you might decide against bullfoot soup, don't miss papaya soup, a memorable dish from Tortola. It is also worth searching for *tannia* (sometimes called *tannier)* soup, based on a Caribbean root vegetable and including cheese, potatoes, carrots, and bacon. Cucumber soup is more common, as is thick, hearty black bean soup. And there's a happy surfeit of fresh seafood soups and chowders to whet the appetite.

Sumptuous sea-fare is always on the menu. Here, wining and dining at Lime Inn Restaurant, Cruz Bay.

Main Courses

No main dish is more typically West Indian than *callaloo*. This fragrant, soupy stew normally includes seasoned pork, salt meat, fresh fish, crab, or conch, okra, spinach or other greens, onions, and garlic. Down island, in the Caribbean, it is also called *pepperpot*.

Complementing local gumbos and stews are pieces of *fungi* (pronounced "foon-jee"), which is a sort of polenta consisting of cornmeal boiled with okra. *Roti* was brought from Trinidad and combines a slightly spicy filling of meat, seafood and/or vegetables with an unleavened soft bread wrapping rather like a tortilla. *Goat water* is a fragrant liquid concoction of goat meat boiled with brown flour, onions, cloves, thyme, garlic,

Try these for size! A lobster fisherman shows off the catch of the day at Anegada.

and celery. It's not to be confused with *stew goat,* which is much drier and has no brown flour.

Throughout the Virgin Islands, fishermen still sell lobster relatively cheaply at the wharf. However, after the short trip from the dock to the restaurant kitchen, the price tends to rise dramatically. Unlike their cold-water cousins, these Caribbean crustaceans don't have claws, and sophisticates say they're really saltwater crayfish. You'll be served either of two types: the spiny or rock lobster (a nocturnal feeder) or the less-common Spanish or slipper lobster (which ventures out in daytime; you can see it if you're diving). Normally, they'll be served grilled, although Puerto Rican-influenced chefs also chop them up as the featured ingredient in a soupy rice stew called an *asopao.*

Widely admired for its magnificent shell, the conch (pronounced "conk") deserves your attention at the dinner table as well. This ubiquitous mollusk appears not only in soups, chowders, and salads, but also as a main dish. You might hear tales about the conch's powers as an aphrodisiac.

Fish can be found in abundant variety. The catch of the day might be red snapper, kingfish, bonito, tuna, or mahi-mahi, but it will always be fresh and delicious. It is served simply, either grilled or with a variety of sauces. Stewed fish, a dish seen on many menus in local restaurants, is simply fish cooked in a small amount of liquid, normally with onions and seasonings; in other parts of the Caribbean it is known as *court bouillon*.

Side Dishes

Vegetables might be white sweet potato, breadfruit, okra, squash, christophene, cassava root, or taro. They're cooked and usually served without frills. Rice 'n' peas is also a popular accompaniment to many dishes. With fish you should be served johnnycake, absolutely delicious when straight out of the oven but uninspiring when cold. This is a sort of dumpling whose original name was *journey cake;* wives used to make a batch for their husbands going out for a long day's work in the fields.

Around the islands, there are literally dozens of variations of native seasoning used in meat and fish dishes, soups, and stews. Local chutneys, pickles, and sauces come in great variety. You can also buy your favorites to take home. Be forewarned: a few drops of liquid pepper sauce (red or yellow) will add a zing to any dish; more than that might well spoil it for you.

Fruits and Desserts

Banana fans will discover that seven varieties grow on the islands. You'll also find papaya, tamarind, sea grapes, mango, and—of course—coconut. Refreshing drinks are made from many of these fruits. Some also go into an array of tantalizing pies, tarts, and cakes.

International Cuisine

For those who prefer the safety of familiar fare, the Virgin Islands will not disappoint. All the islands have plenty of choice when it comes to burgers, steaks, and chicken dishes. Salads abound and pizzas appear on menus with increasing regularity. This is particularly true on St. Thomas, where the fast food chains will delight those who are feeling a bit homesick.

Coladas reign supreme at the cocktail hour…or at any hour, for that matter!

What to Drink

Rum, you might say, makes the West Indies go 'round. It should indeed work that way on you if you try to sample each of the punches, daiquiris, flips, sours, and fizzes created by island bartenders. Cruzan and Pusser's rums are the local products. Many visitors get no further than the piña colada, available anywhere there's a blender. This beguiling confection consists of rum, coconut cream, crushed pineapple (or juice), and crushed ice.

You'll find coconut, banana, peach, and strawberry daiquiris at most bars, and the vast selection of alcoholic creations, even in modest bars, is dizzying. Wines travel from Chile and the US, less so from Europe (except in the finer restaurants, where the prices reflect the cost of importation).

Beer connoisseurs can enjoy some of Europe's and America's best brews but can also try two local brews, both produced on St. Croix. Blackbeard's Ale, a bottled dark beer, hoppy and refreshing, can be found all over the USVI. There is also a microbrewery at King's Alley in Christiansted that produces an excellent, unfiltered beer not for export or sale but only for the brewery's own bar.

Older islanders still drink *maubi,* a drink made of tree bark, ginger, rosemary, sweet marjoram, sugar, and pineapple skin. Although nonalco-

Pirate's choice: Blackbeard's Ale is an excellent local brew.

holic, it's said to pack a punch when aged. Papaya creole combines papaya pulp, chopped bananas, guavas, and lime and cherry juices. Fruit nectars and juices are found in all the usual forms. For a pure and different refreshment, try tamarind juice.

The coffee scene in the islands will be instantly familiar to Americans, the tea situation less so. Bush tea, which is many things to many people in the West Indies, might be made of the *soursop* fruit. This has a flavor midway between a banana and a pineapple, according to one description. It's also claimed to be the only certain cure in the world for a hangover, which—when you consider the number of daiquiris around—is not a bad thing to know.

HANDY TRAVEL TIPS

An A–Z Summary of Practical Information

A

ACCOMMODATION

In the Virgin Islands you'll find a full range of choices, from beach cottages and guesthouses to luxurious all-inclusive hotels. You can stay in a deluxe resort or in a beachside condo; time-shares, vacation homes, and villas are also available. And if you want a room that floats, you can even rent a boat as your temporary home.

By far the largest category of accommodation is the "resort," of which both the USVI and BVI have an abundance in a variety of styles. When making your reservations, you will want to determine the room/meal plan that is best for you. Here are the basic options.

AI: All-Inclusive, with all sporting facilities, resort activities, meals, and drinks included in the room rate.

AP: American Plan, with breakfast, lunch, and dinner included.

MAP: Modified American Plan, providing breakfast and dinner.

EP: European Plan, which is the price for room only.

Although some resorts and hotels include a full range of sporting activities in the price, others charge for every activity, so it is important to check exactly what is included in the basic price before making a confirmed booking. Although All-Inclusive hotels offer all facilities for one price, the quality of the facilities does vary from place to place. Some AI packages still make extra charges for certain activities or for "luxury" food and premium brands of beverages.

Most of the larger hotels on the US islands generally have all the expected amenities, though some of the largest and most expensive try to provide a "get-away-from-it-all" experience without phone, TV, or air-conditioning. Always make sure that you inquire before booking.

In the British islands, renowned for understated luxury, one should not take for granted that the best hotels will have the typical amenities. These resorts pride themselves on their "less-is-more" atmosphere and definitely will not include TV or phone. They might not have air-conditioning, relying on fans and cooling sea breezes to keep the temperature down and on mosquito nets to keep the bugs at bay—this is also much more romantic.

The United States Virgin Islands Department of Tourism produces *Where to Stay,* a leaflet giving details for all hotels and guesthouses on each of the islands for price comparisons. The British Virgin Islands Tourist Board produces a directory with similar information. It is important to make reservations to guarantee the accommodation of your choice, especially in the winter (between November and April).

AIRPORTS

There are three major international airports serving the Virgin Islands: two in the USVI and one in the BVI.

In the USVI, the Henry E. Rohlsen Airport operates on St. Croix and the Cyril E. King Airport (just west of Charlotte Amalie on St. Thomas) serves St. Thomas and St. John. Rohlsen Airport is served by taxis that speed visitors to the hotels in Christiansted and beyond; prices start at around $15. King Airport also has numerous taxis into Charlotte Amalie and out to the east coast of St. Thomas; the cost to eastern hotels and to Red Hook (for the ferry to St. John) is $10.

The only international airport in the BVI is Beef Island Airport, on Tortola. Virgin Gorda has a short strip used by small commercial planes and small private and charter jets. Many visitors to the British islands fly into St. Thomas for onward transportation by commercial ferry or transfer boat.

Those traveling from San Juan or St. Thomas to Beef Island Airport in the BVI will frequently find their luggage left behind, only to arrive the next day with profuse apologies. To be safe rather than sorry, always pack some essentials in your carry-on luggage to tide you over the first 24 hours should you be so unfortunate.

BUDGETING for YOUR TRIP

The Virgin Islands can be an expensive destination because of the abundance of fine hotels and the necessity for importing much of the islands' food. On the other hand, there is no sales tax in either the USVI or the BVI, which makes many premium goods an extremely good value. Here are some sample prices to help with budgeting.

Accommodation. Room rates range from slightly under $100 to over $450 per night.

Hotel charges. Most USVI hotels add a 15 percent service charge to room and restaurant bills; an 8 percent tax applies to hotel rooms. In the BVI, there is a 7 percent hotel accommodation tax, and many hotels will add an extra 10 percent to 12 percent service charge to any bills automatically (be sure to check on this policy); there is no sales tax on BVI hotels.

Food. Meals can run from $25 to over $100 per person, without drinks.

Car rental. Daily rates start at around $40 up to around $90 for larger cars.

Sample taxi fares (per person in private cabs). Charlotte Amalie to Red Hook $9; from King Airport to Red Hook or the eastern hotels $10; Charlotte Amalie to Magen's Bay $4; on Tortola, West End to Road Town $7; Beef Island Airport to Road Town $10; on Virgin Gorda, Spanish Town to the Baths $5. For sightseeing in the USVI with a taxi, you'll pay about $15 per hour for up to 2 people; each extra passenger pays $12. In the BVI, sightseeing is $20 per hour for up to 6 people.

Ferries. One-way trips run from $3 to $7; longer rides are $22–$45.

Diving. Two-tank dives from around $70.

Boat rental. Daily charters for $60 for a small dinghy to $800 for a large fishing boat; weekly bare-boat charters start from around $1500 and depend on the season and the size of boat.

Golf. Green fees $100 per person at Mahogany Run on St. Thomas.

C

CAMPING

Camping is very popular among those wanting to enjoy the natural pleasures of St. John. There are two major campsites in the national park: one at Cinnamon Bay, the other at Maho Bay. Camping is forbidden in other areas of the park, and this makes the campgrounds extremely popular.

Cinnamon Bay is the more basic, but it also has a few cottages. There are complete sites set up for you or bare sites where you can bring your own gear (tel: 340/776-6330; fax: 340/776-6458). Maho Bay is an eco-friendly campground where each unit is 256 sq ft (24 sq m), with some necessities for cooking provided (tel: 340/776-6240, 800-392-9004 toll-free in the US and Canada; fax: 776-6504; website: www.maho.org).

In the BVI there are small campsites on Tortola, Jost Van Dyke, and Anegada: Brewers Bay Campground, Brewers Bay, Tortola (tel: 284/494-3463); White Bay Campground, White Bay, Jost Van Dyke (tel: 284/495-9312); Anegada Beach Campground (tel: 284/495-9466); Mac's Place Camping, Anegada (tel: 284/495-8020).

CAR RENTAL

It is possible—and useful—to rent a car on St. Thomas, St. John, St. Croix, Tortola, and Virgin Gorda. Drivers must be over 21 and carry a valid driver's license; some smaller companies stipulate a minimum age of 25. If you are not from the US, a USVI driver's license will automatically be issued on production of your own valid license and will be valid for 90 days. In the BVI, those renting a car will pay $10 for a temporary BVI driver's license on production of a valid license from their own country.

All rental agreements offer damage waiver and personal insurance as extras. Check your own policy to find out if you are already covered; if not, it would be wise to take out this optional cover to limit your liability in case of an accident.

Most of the major international rental companies have offices in the USVI and BVI. There are also local companies with very competitive rates, but do inquire about the condition of the vehicle before making your reservation.

You should make a reservation well before your arrival if you visit during peak season. Daily charges start at around $50, up to $80 in high season.

CLIMATE and CLOTHING

Climate. The Virgin Islands have, in general, one of the finest year-round climates anywhere. The temperature in the USVI stays around 80°F (27°C), and the trade winds keep the weather warm and appealing but not hot and stifling. The "rainy season," though it hardly merits the name, is officially in the fall. Showers are capricious. Rainfall averages approximately 40 inches (100 cm) per year, coming mostly in brief showers at night.

The official hurricane season is from 1 June to 30 November. However, forecasters can now locate storms thousands of miles away, giving local people and visitors ample time to leave the islands if danger threatens.

Approximate monthly averages for the USVI are indicated below, the BVI temperatures reach 80°F in the winter and 84°F in the summer. The ocean water is usually just a few degrees higher than the air temperature, and the water stays even warmer in the winter.

Average Air temperature:

	J	F	M	A	M	J	J	A	S	O	N	D
°F	77	77	78	78	79	81	82	82	81	80	78	76
°C	25	25	25	25	26	27	28	28	27	27	25	24

Clothing. You should have no trouble packing a wardrobe for your trip to the Virgin Islands. Beach attire is a must, plus comfortable wraps or cover-ups for relaxing around the hotel. Don't wear anything too skimpy if you head into town. Instead, wear T-shirt and shorts (for both sexes), or women can wear a summer dress. Local people do not admire a bare chest on men or midriff on women. Bring something a little more formal for evening, perhaps, but the Virgin Islands do not generally require formal dress for dinner (although if you book into one of the finer hotels, ask whether they have a dress code). In the BVI things are even less stringent. Around the marinas many people don't bother to change for dinner, preferring a totally relaxed holiday.

Light cottons or silks make the best fabrics, being breathable and cool. Don't forget a hat, sunglasses, and sunscreen, because the sun is very strong here. Those who intend to go hiking on St. John or other islands should have sturdy shoes and long-sleeved, lightweight shirts to guard against sunburn and insects.

COMPLAINTS

Complaints should always be taken up first with the establishment or individual concerned. If this is unsuccessful, then take your complaint to the main tourist office on the island you are visiting. They should be able to advise you further.

CRIME and SAFETY

Crime has been rising in the USVI, but the facts show that most of the major crime is not aimed at visitors but exists within the community—often with the young and often drug-related. This does not mean that once on vacation you should abandon common sense. Always take sensible precautions. Never carry large amounts of cash or valuables; use the hotel or cruise-ship safe. Travel well-lit streets at night, in a group if possible. Use official taxis only, and do not accept lifts from someone who stops to offer you one. Put all valuables out of sight when leaving your vehicle; even better, take them with you. Always park in a well-frequented lot or street. Do not leave valuables on the beach when you go for a swim.

The BVI are regarded as some of the safest tourist destinations in the world, and major crime is almost unknown. Most local people leave houses and cars unlocked when they leave them. Even petty crime such as theft is at a low level. However, this does not absolve the visitor from taking the same basic precautions with any valuables they carry.

CUSTOMS and ENTRY REGULATIONS

Entering the USVI. Travelers from the US and Canada require only some form of photo identification to travel to the islands. Those traveling from other countries through the US will be required to clear immigration before entering the US. This means carrying a valid passport and obtaining a visa for travel (or filling in a green card under the visa waiver scheme). Visitors from the UK need a valid passport and green visa waiver form to enter. For foreign visitors, items for personal use can be brought in duty-free. The head of each family group must also complete a customs declaration form. Customs ask that you declare cash valued at more than $10,000. Visitors from the continental

US or Puerto Rico do not need to pass through customs when entering the USVI.

Entering the BVI. Visitors from the British Commonwealth and the EU need only a valid passport to be admitted for up to 90 days. Those planning to stay for longer than a day must have pre-arranged lodgings. Citizens of the US and Canada will have few difficulties if they carry a valid passport when they enter the BVI, but carrying birth or naturalization certificate and some form of picture ID will do. (The BVI will not allow entrance to those it deems "hippies" or Rastafarians. What this means exactly is unclear, since there is a Rastafarian church on Virgin Gorda.) All arrivals to the BVI must travel through customs; items for personal use can be brought in duty-free.

Customs exemptions. When visiting the US Virgin Islands, each American citizen regardless of age can purchase $1,200 in goods every 40 days without being charged duty when returning home. This means that a couple on holiday with their young child can take home $3,600 worth of goods before duty becomes payable. For citizens of Canada, the limit on goods purchased in the USVI is C$300; for the UK, £136; for Australia, A$200; for New Zealand, NZ$700.

For the BVI, the limit on duty-free purchases by US citizens is $600. Limits for citizens of other nations are similar to those listed above for the USVI.

It is always best to check with your government's customs agency before your trip to determine the exact limits in effect on shopping purchases.

D

DRIVING

Rules and regulations. Throughout the Virgin Islands—both British and US—driving is on the *left side of the road*. This is especially confusing for American visitors to the USVI, who expect right-side driving in this US territory. Most accidents involve visiting tourists who pull out from a junction onto the wrong side of the road and into the path of an oncoming vehicle.

Speed limits are low: around 20 mph (32 km/h) in town and 35 mph (56 km/h) in the countryside. Be forewarned that drivers on Tortola tend to ignore speed limits.

In the USVI, left turns are permitted at a red light (after stopping first) unless otherwise indicated. Right-hand turns are *not* permitted at a red light because you would be crossing a lane of traffic.

Road conditions. Street and road conditions are reasonable in all the USVI, although some of the roadways are narrow and twist and turn constantly. Take things slowly and deliberately at difficult junctions. Road conditions are not as good in the BVI, but they are certainly acceptable. Drivers throughout the Virgin Islands will stop without warning or signaling in order to chat with friends or offer a lift to someone walking along. Always be prepared for the vehicle ahead of you to do something surprising. On Tortola and Virgin Gorda, watch for stray goats and chickens. Unfortunately, if you need help, there is no national service to come to your aid. Ask your rental agency for a number to call in case of a breakdown, but don't expect someone to come out and rescue you within minutes.

Fuel. Gasoline (petrol) is easy to find on the major islands, and service stations are open daily between the hours of 9am and 5pm. Some have extended hours. Fuel is more expensive than on the US mainland but cheaper than in the UK and Europe.

Parking. It can be difficult to find a parking place in Charlotte Amalie and Christiansted. On most of the islands people are pretty relaxed about things—unless you are blocking an access or are in a dangerous situation. In town, always park away from the yellow lines and yellow raised sidewalks, which indicate no-parking areas.

E

ELECTRICITY

All supplies are 110-volt/60-cycle AC. Travelers from the North American mainland will not need adapters for their appliances. Other visitors will need standard US adapters.

EMBASSIES and CONSULATES

Since both the USVI and BVI are territories, diplomatic assistance is usually found through various nations' embassies and consulates in Washington and London, respectively. There are, however, two local consular offices in Charlotte Amalie, St. Thomas, USVI. The Royal Danish Consulate is in the Scandinavian Center at Havensight Mall, Building 3 (tel: 340/776-0656), and the British Consulate is at 1 Fortets Gade (tel: 340/774-0033).

EMERGENCIES

In the USVI: dial **911**. In the BVI: dial **999**.

For those on boats, there are emergency services on Tortola (radio channel 16) for connections to search-and-rescue providers.

G

GAY and LESBIAN TRAVELERS

Although there are no organizations in the islands, there is a casual but growing gay and lesbian community in Frederiksted on St. Croix, where you will find some guesthouses and hotels as well as bars. The latter include On the Beach and the Last Hurrah. For further information, contact a knowledgeable gay and lesbian travel agency serving the Caribbean through the International Gay and Lesbian Travel Association in Ft. Lauderdale, Florida (tel: 800-448-8550 toll-free in the US and Canada; website: www.iglta.org).

GETTING THERE

By air. St. Thomas, St. Croix, and Tortola have international airports (see AIRPORTS), with St. Thomas serving as the airport of entry for St. John and often for the British Virgin Islands as well.

Direct flights to St. Thomas can be made from Miami, New York (JFK), Atlanta, and Philadelphia. Frequent connections can also be made through San Juan, Puerto Rico. For travel to St. Croix, flights originate in Miami, Atlanta, and Philadelphia; again, frequent connections are available through San Juan.

Virgin Islands

There are no non-stop flights from the US mainland to the British Virgin Islands. Instead, all flights to Beef Island Airport on Tortola originate in San Juan, Puerto Rico, or in St. Thomas, USVI.

European visitors to the Virgin Islands must transfer at one of the major US hub cities or at San Juan to reach the islands. British Airways has flights to the US (New York and Miami) and San Juan for onward connection to the USVI and then the BVI.

By sea. All three US Virgin Islands are on the cruise ship itinerary, with St. Thomas one of the world's major cruise destinations. Several cruise lines make stops at Road Town, Tortola (BVI), with onward excursions to Virgin Gorda.

Celebrity Cruises: tel: 800-722-5941 (toll-free in US) and tel: 0800-018-2525 (in UK).

Norwegian Cruise Line: tel: 800-327-7030 (toll-free in US) and tel: 0800-181-560 (toll-free in UK).

Royal Caribbean International: tel: 800-327-6700 (toll-free in US) and tel: 0800-018-2020 (toll-free in UK).

GUIDES and TOURS

On St. Thomas, the Virgin Islands Taxi Association offers a two-hour island tour (tel: 340/774-7457). On St. Croix, Eagle Safari Tours will provide day-tours Monday–Saturday throughout the island for groups or private charters (tel: 340/778-3313; fax: 340/773-1672). On Tortola, the BVI Taxi Association provides tours (tel: 284/494-2875).

H

HEALTH and MEDICAL CARE

Each of the islands has a clinic or medical center for emergency care or noncritical conditions, including a decompression chamber at the hospital in St. Thomas for diving accidents. However, for serious or critical conditions, patients are transported to San Juan or Miami for treatment. Contact details are as follows:

Roy L. Schneider Hospital (near Charlotte Amalie, St. Thomas; tel: 340/776-8311).

Governor Juan F. Luis Hospital (just north of the Sunny Isles Shopping Center, St. Croix; tel: 340/778-6311).

Myrah Keating Smith Community Health Center (St. John; tel: 340/693-8900).

Peebles Hospital (Road Town, Tortola; tel: 284/494-3497).

Emergency patients on Virgin Gorda will be transferred to Tortola or St. Thomas so that a diagnosis can be made and an appropriate course of action taken. There are two clinics on the island, one at Spanish Town and one at North Sound.

You will have to pay the cost of transfers from outlying islands to reach medical attention. Always make sure you carry adequate insurance to cover any medical problem you might have while on vacation.

General precautions. The Virgin Islands are generally healthy and safe places to vacation, provided that you take a few sensible precautions. First, start your tanning slowly to avoid sunburn and sunstroke. The islands are very close to the equator (where the sun is strongest), and sea breezes that blow across the islands can lull you into a sense of false security. Use a good sunscreen. And go easy on the alcohol —especially in the sunshine—as this could lead to dehydration.

There are some minor nuisances that should be avoided. Mosquitoes can be a problem, particularly in St. John and all the British islands. As the sun begins to set, cover up or apply insect repellent and use screens on patio windows. Called "no see 'ems" by the locals because they are so small, sandflies can also bite. Carry repellent with you at all times just in case you come across them. The manchineel tree has a poisonous bark and can be caustic even if you stand under it in a rainstorm; take care to avoid it (there are signs posted near many trees).

Don't step on spiny sea urchins when you snorkel or dive, as the spines will embed themselves in your flesh and can become infected. Do not touch any creatures or coral under the water because some are toxic. Don't pick up large hermit crabs, which can give you a nasty nip!

HOLIDAYS

Virgin Islanders could very well have more official days off than anybody else in the world, although not every institution is closed on every holiday. The following are public holidays in the USVI, the BVI, or both:

Virgin Islands

1 January	*New Year's Day*
6 January	*Three Kings Day (ends the 12-day St. Croix Christmas carnival)*
15 January	*Martin Luther King Jr. birthday (USVI)*
February	*Presidents' Day (third Monday, USVI)*
31 March	*Transfer Day (USVI)*
March	*Commonwealth Day (second Monday, BVI)*
March/April	*Holy Thursday; Good Friday; Easter Monday*
May	*Memorial Day (last Monday, USVI)*
20 June	*Organic Act Day (USVI)*
June	*Queen's Birthday (second Monday, BVI)*
1 July	*Territory Day (BVI)*
3 July	*Emancipation Day (USVI)*
4 July	*American Independence Day (USVI)*
July	*Hurricane Supplication Day*
August	*BVI Festival (closings on first Monday, Tuesday, and Wednesday)*
September	*Labor Day (first Monday, USVI)*
12 October	*Columbus Day*
17 October	*Hurricane Thanksgiving Day*
21 October	*St. Ursula's Day (BVI)*
1 November	*Liberty Day*
11 November	*Veterans' Day (USVI)*
November	*Thanksgiving Day (fourth Thursday, USVI)*
25 December	*Christmas Day*
26 December	*Christmas Second Day (USVI)/Boxing Day (BVI)*

L

LANGUAGE

English is the language of the Virgin Islands, where it is spoken with a Caribbean flavor. Local people are said to speak English with a "calypso" lilt.

Spanish is spoken by approximately 45 percent of the population of St. Croix. Also on St. Croix—where the colonial Danish influence is still strong—you will hear many English-speaking Danes.

MAPS

For the USVI, an official roadmap, produced by the government, is very comprehensive, with detailed maps of the major towns on each of the islands. It is available at tourist information offices. There is no commercial input on this map. However, there are several maps produced by businesses on the islands, showing where the major shops and restaurants are located. These can be found in hotel lobbies and shopping mall information kiosks.

The British Virgin Islands Tourist Board and Hotel and Commerce Association produce the *Welcome Tourist Guide,* an 84-page information pack with a map of all the BVI in the center. This is probably sufficient for many short-term visitors, but not for those renting a car on Tortola or Virgin Gorda. Car rental companies will issue more detailed maps when you pick up your car.

You can also find maps of varying quality on the many websites devoted to the Virgin Islands (see TOURIST INFORMATION).

MEDIA

The USVI have three daily newspapers: the *Virgin Islands Daily News* and the *Independent,* both on St. Thomas, and the *St. Croix Avis.* Newspapers from New York, Miami, and San Juan arrive daily and are readily available, along with *USA Today.* For visitors there are additional sources of local information. The most comprehensive are *St. Croix This Week* and *St. Thomas This Week* (the latter including St. John). They give a comprehensive overview of activities taking place during your stay, and you'll find them at the airport and information kiosks as well as in hotel lobbies.

The BVI have three weekly newspapers, the *Island Sun,* published Friday, the *BVI Standpoint,* and the *BVI Beacon* published Thursday. Visitors should be sure to pick up a copy of the *Limin' Times* to get an up-to-date picture of what's happening during their time in Tortola or Virgin Gorda.

There is a wide choice of radio stations including: ZBVI on 780khz on AM; FM stations: Gem 90.9mhz (urban and reggae music, Z-Wave 97.3mhz (reggae), Z-Hit 94.3mhz (country), Z-Gold 91.7mhz (Caribbean and calypso), and ZROD 103.7mhz.

Depending on where you stay, your hotel might or might not have television. Cable includes all the major US networks, along with Spanish-language channels.

MONEY MATTERS

Currency. Both the US and British Virgin Islands use the US dollar as their currency.

Banks. There are more banks on the major islands (St. Thomas, St. Croix, and Tortola), and in their large towns, than on the smaller ones. On other islands and smaller towns on these main islands there are banks, but opening times might be rather inconvenient. USVI banks are open Monday–Thursday 9am–3pm and Friday 9am–4:30pm. BVI banks are open Monday–Friday 9am–3pm.

Credit cards. Major credit cards are accepted in most establishments (including shops and restaurants), although some local bars and restaurants in the BVI accept cash only. There are sometimes glitches with the machines and phone lines for credit card verification, but these are part of the fabric of relaxed island life.

ATMS. There are international ATMS in downtown Charlotte Amalie, Christiansted, and Road Town. Not all Virgin Islands banks are linked to such major systems as Cirrus, Plus, and Star, so be sure to check first. Most ATMS will accept major credit cards for cash withdrawal.

Traveler's checks. Most establishments accept traveler's checks. Some banks will charge a premium to cash them, particularly in the BVI. Always carry US dollar denominations rather than checks in another currency.

O

OPENING HOURS

Shops are usually open 9am–6pm, although some have extended hours. Many shops are closed on Sunday, even in the main tourist centers. Government offices are open from 9am–5pm.

Museums and tourist attractions are generally open from 9am to 5pm daily, and many are closed on major holidays.

P

POLICE

In the US Virgin Islands **911** is the standard emergency telephone number. Police presence can be seen most clearly on St. Thomas, where police cars make regular patrols. In the BVI the emergency number is **999**.

POST OFFICES

Post offices are open Monday–Friday from 8:30am to 4:30pm and on Saturday from 8am to noon.

The postal service in the USVI is linked with the US mainland, and service takes only a couple of days longer than from mainland destinations. The BVI also use this system, so that post from Tortola or Virgin Gorda will take at least another day (probably longer) to reach its destination.

Post offices can be found at the corner of Main Street and Tolbod Gade and in Havensight Mall (both in Charlotte Amalie, St. Thomas), in the historic center on Company Street in Christiansted (St. Croix), next to the tourist information center in Cruz Bay (St. John), at the Virgin Gorda Yacht Club (Virgin Gorda), and on Main Street (Tortola). Hotels will also accept your mail.

Postage is the same on both sets of islands. Regular postcards to the US cost $0.20; postcards to other destinations are $0.50.

Virgin Islands

PUBLIC TRANSPORTATION

Buses. Many islanders use buses to and from work. In the USVI, there are public bus systems on each of the islands; in the BVI, only Tortola has buses. The vehicles are frequently overcrowded, and they make many stops en route to their final destinations. Air-conditioning is often not in the best condition. But if leisurely sightseeing filled with local color appeals to you, then you might want to try a short bus trip to experience this mode of transport. It is certainly very inexpensive.

VITRAN operates the public bus system on St. Thomas, St. Croix, and St. John. Modern buses and minivans have regularly scheduled routes with clearly marked stops. The fare is generally $1 anywhere on an island, with city routes within Charlotte Amalie priced at $0.75. There are lower rates for seniors. For schedule information, contact VITRAN: St. Thomas (tel: 340/774-5678); St. Croix (tel: 340/773-7746); St. John (tel: 340/776-6346).

On Tortola in the BVI, Scato's Bus Service (tel: 284/494-2365) operates minivans that take passengers directly to their destinations. There are no scheduled pickup spots and no set fares.

Taxis. These typically will be waiting at airports and ferry ports. You can also call a taxi to pick you up at your hotel. In the USVI taxi fares are posted and standard; your driver should have a list of fares in the vehicle. Prices are lower if there are two or more passengers. In the BVI there is no standardized list of fares, so agree on a price before you depart. Prices in the British islands appear to be similar to those in the USVI, although the vehicles are a little older. For sample taxi fares around the islands, see BUDGETING FOR YOUR TRIP.

For less expensive taxi service, most islands have minivans and open-air "Safari" vans that stop at stands in every major town and cruise the streets for passengers. The drivers will often load up with passengers before taking him or her to his or her destination. This means your trip might be much longer than were you to have your own taxi. But fares are quite low: for example, $1.50 between Christiansted and Frederiksted on St. Croix (with many stops along the way). Again, if you value local color and meeting Virgin Islanders—and don't mind a bit of inconvenience—this is the way to travel.

Ferries. For service via ferry, see page 83.

R

RELIGION

Christianity is the dominant religion throughout the Virgin Islands, with many denominations. St. Croix itself has over 100 churches. Although quite small, there are also—among others—Hindu, Muslim, and Jewish communities in the islands, many originating in colonial times when traders and merchants settled here from Europe, Africa, Asia, and the Americas.

Sundays are regarded as a day of rest, with many shops and businesses closed for the day, but this practice is changing on the main islands. Restaurants, however, do not ordinarily close on Sundays.

T

TELEPHONE

When calling the Virgin Islands from abroad, always dial the access code (1) before the number.

You must also know whether your party is in the United States Virgin Islands or in the British Virgin Islands. The area code for all the USVI is 340. The area code for all the BVI is 284. Dial the seven-digit phone number after dialing (1) plus the appropriate area code.

International and long-distance telephone calls from the Virgin Islands (and particularly the BVI) are exorbitantly expensive, so it pays to be prepared if you need to make some calls. Always ask about the price of calls from your hotel before you make any; the cost (including hotel service charges) might be a shock. Try not to make long-distance calls from your hotel room.

You will find public phones that link directly to USADirect and to AT&T. You can then charge calls to your major credit card. AT&T also has a phone center at Havensight Mall near the cruise port in Charlotte Amalie. All US phone cards will operate in the USVI.

Most US cards will not be accepted in phones in the BVI. It is best to check with your card supplier before you leave. Caribbean Phone Cards are available in denominations of $5, $10, and $20. They can be used all over the Caribbean and are available from hotels and stores.

Virgin Islands

TIME ZONES

All islands are in the Atlantic Time Zone. This is one hour ahead of the Eastern Time Zone in the US and four hours behind GMT. The Virgin Islands do not observe Daylight Savings Time; in the summer months, island time is the same as Eastern Daylight Time. The following chart shows times in winter:

San Francisco	New York	**Virgin Islands**	London	Sydney
8am	11am	**noon**	4pm	2am

TIPPING

Many hotels and restaurants will automatically add gratuities to your bill and will indicate this practice on menus and other literature. For restaurants that do not add a service or gratuity charge, it is customary to leave 15 percent of the total. You should also leave 15 percent for taxi drivers and for maid service.

TOILETS

In general, public toilets are kept clean and in good condition. However, many are located at or near public beaches and, as a result, might be sandy with wet floors by the end of the day. Note that the water found at beaches and other public sites should be used only for washing. Around the islands, there are facilities at the following locations:

St. John. There are free public toilets in Cruz Bay (opposite the tourist information office), at Mongoose Junction Mall, and at Trunk Bay and Cinnamon Bay beaches.

St. Thomas. There are free public toilets at Magen's Bay Beach and at Mountain Top.

St. Croix. You will find toilets in Fort Christiansvaern.

Tortola. Public facilities at the vendors' market on the waterfront.

Virgin Gorda. There are public toilets at the Virgin Gorda Yacht Club, at the Leverick Bay marina, and at the Baths.

TOURIST INFORMATION

USVI. For information before you leave home, contact the US Virgin Islands Department of Tourism offices at the following addresses.

Atlanta: 245 Peachtree Center Ave., Marquis One Tower, Atlanta GA 30303; tel: (404) 688-0906; fax: (404) 525-1102.

Chicago: 500 N. Michigan Ave., Suite 2030, Chicago IL 60611; tel. (312) 670-8784; fax: (312) 670-8788.

Los Angeles: 3460 Wilshire Blvd., Suite 412, Los Angeles CA 90010; tel. (213) 739-0138; fax: (213) 739-2005.

Miami: 2655 South LeJeune Rd., Suite 907, Coral Gables FL 33134; tel: (305) 442-7200; fax: (305) 445-9044.

New York City: 1270 Avenue of the Americas, Suite 2108, New York NY 10020; tel: (212) 332-2222; fax: (212) 332-2223.

Washington DC: 444 North Capital St. NW, Suite 305, Washington DC 20001; tel: (202) 624-3590; fax: (202) 624-3594.

San Juan, Puerto Rico: 268 Ponce de Leon Ave., Suite 1101, Hato Rey, Puerto Rico 00918; tel: (787) 763-3815; fax: (787) 763-3890.

Canada: 703 Evans Ave., Suite 106, Toronto, Ontario M9C 5E9; tel: (416) 622-7600; fax: 622-3431.

UK: Power Road Studios, 114 Power Road, London W4 5PY; tel: 020 8994-9848; fax: 020 8994-0962.

In the islands, USVI tourist information offices are located at:
St. Thomas: Tolbod Gade (across street from Emancipation Park), Charlotte Amalie; tel: (340) 774-8784; fax: (340) 774-4390.

St. John: center of town in Cruz Bay; tel: (340) 776 6450; fax: (340) 776-6450.

St. Croix: 53-A Company Street, Christiansted; tel: (340) 773-0495; fax: (340) 773-5074.

BVI. For information before you leave home contact the British Virgin Islands Tourist Board at the following addresses. In the US and Canada, a toll-free phone number is available; tel: 800-835-8530.

Atlanta: 3400 Peachtree Rd. NE, Suite 1735, Lenox Towers, Atlanta GA 30326; tel: (404) 467-4741; fax: (404) 467-4342.

Los Angeles: 3450 Wilshire Blvd., Suite 1202, Los Angeles CA 90010; tel: (213) 736-8931; fax: (213) 736-8935.

New York: 370 Lexington Ave., New York NY 10017; Tel (212) 696-0400; fax: (212) 949-8254.

Virgin Islands

San Francisco: 1804 Union St., San Francisco CA 94123;
tel: (415) 775-0344; fax: (415) 775-2554.

UK: BVI Tourist Board, Banks Hoggins O'Shea FCB, 55 Newman
Street, London W1P 3PG; tel: 020 7947-8200; fax: 020 7947-8279.

In the islands, BVI tourist information offices are located at:
Tortola: Akara Building (2nd floor), Wickham's Cay 1, Road Town;
tel: (284) 494-3134; fax: (284) 494-3866. There is also a small office
on the waterfront at Smith's Ferry, Road Town; tel: (284) 494-7260.
Virgin Gorda: Virgin Gorda Yacht Club, Spanish Town;
tel: (284) 495-5181.

Internet information. Following is list of some useful websites to
help you plan your trip:
USVI: <www.virginisles.com>, <www.usvi.net>,
<www.st-croix.com>, <www.st-thomas.com>, <www.st-john.com>,
<www.virgin.islands.national-park.com>.
BVI: <www.bviwelcome.com>, <www.britishvirginislands.com>,
<www.islandsonline.com>, <www.bvi.org>.

W
WEIGHTS and MEASURES

The US and the British islands use American/Imperial measurements
for distances, weights, liquid measure, and temperature.

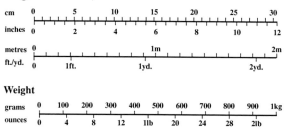

Recommended Hotels

(For further details about hotels in the Virgin Islands, see ACCOMMODATION, page 111.)

There is a broad range of accommodations in the Virgin Islands, but the emphasis is definitely at the upper end of the scale—both in style and price. More modest facilities can be found in small guesthouses or family-run hotels, and some historic houses have been converted into hotels offering a "colonial feel." There is very little choice in the budget sector of the market, with prices usually higher than in mainland US hotels.

The British islands tend to cater to those looking for expensive retreats, with few formal activities; some do not even have such amenities as TV and in-room phone. The US resort hotels, in contrast, will often have a full range of water sports and other planned activities, along with more in-room amenities. Many hotels welcome children and have special programs for them, but others have a policy of not catering to young children.

Unless otherwise stated, standard features include air-conditioning, color cable TV, clock radio, fridge or minibar, coffee-making facilities, hairdryer, iron and ironing board, and wall safe.

The price ranges quoted are in US dollars. Many hotels will add a service charge of 10 percent to 15 percent, and in the British islands there is an occupancy tax of 7 percent. Remember that prices can vary enormously between high and low season (winter generally being the most expensive).

$$$$	above $350
$$$	$250–$350
$$	$170–$250
$	$100–$170

UNITED STATES VIRGIN ISLANDS

Note that all seven-digit local telephone numbers must be preceded by the **340** access code for the USVI when dialing from abroad.

St. Thomas

Hotel 1829 $-$$ *Government Hill, P.O. Box 302579, Charlotte Amalie, St. Thomas, USVI 00804; tel: 776-1829, 800-524-2002 (toll-free in the US); fax: 776-4313; www.hotel1829.com.* Historic Spanish-style hotel built on several levels atop Government Hill, a short walk from downtown. Said to have been frequented by author Graham Greene. One restaurant, atmospheric bar. 14 rooms. Major credit cards.

Marriott Frenchman and Morningstar Resort $$$-$$$$ *Frenchman's Bay, P.O. Box 7100, Charlotte Amalie, St. Thomas, USVI 00801; tel: 776-8500, 800-570-4423 (toll-free in US); fax: 715-6191; www.offshoreresorts.com.* Two hotels combine to create a super-service resort, dramatically located on a promontory east of downtown. Shuttle boat to Charlotte Amalie, six restaurants, four tennis courts, two pools, children's club, and scheduled activities for adults. 517 rooms. Major credit cards.

Point Pleasant Resort $$$ *6600 Estate Smith Bay #4, St. Thomas, USVI 00801; tel: 775-7200, 800-524-2300 (toll-free in US); fax: 776-5694; www.pointpleasantresort.com.* Situated between two white sand beaches, atop a hillside offering spectacular tropical views. Three pools, one tennis court, exercise room. 95 rooms. Major credit cards.

Renaissance Grand Beach Resort $$$ *Smith's Bay Road, P.O. Box 8267, St. Thomas, USVI 00801; tel: 775-1510, 800-HOTELS-1 (toll-free in US); fax: 775-2185; www.renaissancehotels.com.* On a natural bay with fabulous views of Tortola and Jost Van Dyke, only a five-minute walk from Coki Beach and Coral World. Renowned for its diving and watersports facilities. Fine sand beach, two pools, fitness center, two restaurants, floodlit tennis courts, children's club, gift shop, iguanas in the landscaped gardens. Rooms are tiered on hillside. 290 rooms. Major credit cards.

Ritz Carlton $$$$ *6900 Great Bay, St. Thomas, USVI 00802; tel: 775-3333, 800-421-3333 (toll-free in US); fax: 775-4444; www.ritzcarlton.com.* Italianate design and rich fittings are the signature of this hotel set in tropical gardens. Three restaurants, three lit tennis courts, fitness center, spa, iguana feeding sessions, children's club. 152 rooms. Major credit cards.

Sapphire Beach Resort and Marina $$-$$$ *Smith's Bay Road, P.O. Box 8088, St. Thomas, USVI 00801; tel: 775-6100, 800-524-2090 (toll-free in US); www.saphirebeachresort.com.* Located on the white-sand Sapphire Beach, with full marina facilities for 32 slips. Two restaurants, pool, daily live music at the beach bar, children's club. 171 rooms. Major credit cards.

Wyndham Sugar Bay Resort $$$ *6500 Smith's Bay Road, St. Thomas, USVI 00802; tel: 777-7100, 800-927-7100 (toll-free in US); fax: 777-7200.* A large all-inclusive hotel set in manicured grounds on a high promontory overlooking Smith's Bay, with great views across Pillsbury Sound to St. John. A combination of elevators and stairs or shuttle bus take you to boardwalks, a large pool, sundeck, and palm-fringed beach. Two restaurants, water sports, floodlit tennis courts, children's club, gift shop. 300 rooms. Major credit cards.

St. John

Caneel Bay Resort $$$ *Cruz Bay, P.O. Box 720, St. John, USVI 00831; tel: 776-6111, 888-ROSEWOOD (toll-free in US and Canada); fax: 693-8280; www.caneelbay.com.* A well-known "get away from it all" resort with extensive grounds on the famous North Shore. This was the spot established by Laurance Rockefeller in 1955. No TV or phones in rooms. Seven beaches, pool, three restaurants, 11 tennis courts. 166 rooms. Major credit cards.

Cinnamon Bay Campground $ *Cinnamon Bay, P.O. Box 720, St. John, USVI 00831; tel: 776-6330; fax: 776-6458; www.cinnamonbay.com.* This campsite on the Cinnamon Bay beach has a restaurant, although the tents and cottages come with equipped kitchens (grills and picnic tables). 126 units. Major credit cards.

Gallows Point Resort $$-$$$ *P.O. Box 58, St. John, USVI 00831; tel: 776-6434, 800-323-7229 (toll-free in US); fax: 776-6520; www.gallowspointresort.com.* Overlooking Cruz Bay Harbor and Pillsbury Sound and only a five-minute walk from the center of Cruz Bay. All apartments have kitchens and plant-filled showers. 51 rooms. Major credit cards.

Westin Resort $$$$ *Great Cruz Bay, P.O. Box 8310, St. John, USVI 00831; Tel: 693-8000, 800-WESTIN-1, 800-808-5020 (toll-free in US); fax: 693-8510; www.westin.com.* On a hillside alongside a horseshoe-shaped bay and five minutes by car from Cruz Bay, this large hotel has two restaurants, fitness center, dive school, and day cruises onsite. 285 rooms. Major credit cards.

St. Croix

Buccaneer Hotel $$$-$$$$ *Gallows Bay, P.O. Box 25200, Christiansted, St. Croix, USVI 00824; Tel: 712-2100, 800-255-3881 (toll-free in US); fax: 712-2104; www.thebuccaneer.com.* With three palm-fringed beaches and extensive manicured grounds, this hotel (its main building dates back to 1653) is in the *Conde Nast* list of 50 top getaways. Eight tennis courts, 18-hole golf course with views across Gallows Bay, jogging track, two restaurants in the main building, two beachside restaurants. Two miles from downtown. 132 rooms. Major credit cards.

Hilty House $$ *2, Hermon Hill, Gallows Bay, P.O. Box 26077, St. Croix, USVI 00824; tel: 773-2594; fax: 773-2594; e-mail: hiltyhouse@worldnet.att.net.* This historic plantation greathouse is only a few minutes from Christiansted. It's been renovated as a friendly bed-and-breakfast establishment. Pool and sundeck, dinner on Monday evenings in informal "house-party" style. 5 rooms. Major credit cards.

Hotel Caravelle $$ *44a Queen Cross St., Christiansted, St. Croix, USVI 00820; tel: 773-0687, 800-524-0410 (toll-free in US); fax: 778-7004; www.hotelcaravellestcroix.com.* This European-style hotel is situated in the heart of Christiansted, with restaurants and bars close by. Rooms are clean, furnishings tidy. Sun terrace and pool. 43 rooms. Major credit cards.

King's Alley Hotel $$ *57 King Street, P.O. Box 4120, Christiansted, St. Croix, USVI 00822; tel: 773-0103, 800-843-3574 (toll-free in US); fax: 773-4431; www.stcroix.net.* Renovated hotel in Continental style, situated in the heart of Christiansted. Rooms are nicely furnished, some with French windows overlooking King's Alley. 35 rooms. Major credit cards.

Tamarind Reef Hotel $$$ *5001 Tamarind Reef, Christiansted, St. Croix, USVI 00820; tel: 773-4455, 800-619-0014 (toll free in US); fax: 773-3989; www.usvi.net/hotel/tamarind.* Small two-story hotel only ten minutes by car from downtown. Some rooms with kitchenette, views of Buck Island. Pool, café, shop. Space for 180 boats at marina. 45 rooms. Major credit cards.

BRITISH VIRGIN ISLANDS

Note that all seven-digit local phone numbers must be preceded by the **284** access code for the BVI when dialing from abroad.

Tortola

Frenchman's Cay Hotel $$-$$$ *P.O. Box 1054, West End, Tortola, BVI; tel: 495-4844, 800-235-4077 (toll-free in US), 800-463-0199 (toll-free in Canada); fax: 495-4056; www.frenchmans.com.* Overlooking Drake's Channel and only minutes from Soper's Hole on foot, these villas are cooled by the sea breeze. Full kitchens, small pool, artificial beach, alfresco bar and dining room. No TV in rooms. 9 units. Major credit cards.

Lambert Beach Resort $$$ *P.O. Box 534, East End, Tortola, BVI; tel: 495-2877; fax: 495-2876; www.lambertbeachresort.com.* On wide sandy bay in the north of the island, a 20-minute drive from the airport or Road Town. The resort features the largest pool on the island, bar, restaurant, gift shop. No TV in rooms. 38 units. Major credit cards.

Long Bay Beach Resort $$$ *P.O. Box 433, Road Town, Tortola, BVI; tel: 495-4252, 800-729-9599 (toll-free in the US); fax: 495-4677; www.longbay.com.* Located on a hillside overlooking the mile-long arc of Long Bay, with a walking trail to Smuggler's Cove. Beach. Garden restaurants, fitness center, pool, nine-hole golf course, tennis court, gift shop. 82 rooms. Major credit cards.

Sugar Mill Hotel $$-$$$ *P.O. Box 425, Road Town, Tortola, BVI; tel: 495-4355; fax: 495-4696.* On the north coast near Cane Garden Bay. Reception area, bar, and restaurant are situated in the ruins of the old sugar mill. Simply furnished rooms are spread up the hillside in this country atmosphere. Swimming pool, beach, terrace restaurant. No TV in rooms; some with no air-conditioning. 21 rooms. Major credit cards.

Virgin Gorda

Biras Creek Resort $$$ *P.O. Box 54, Virgin Gorda, BVI; tel: 494-3555; fax: 494-3557; e-mail: biras@caribsurf.com.* Situated on a peninsula at North Sound (accessible only by boat), this luxury hotel is featured in many travel magazines. Award-winning restaurant, beautiful beach, bar, pool, two tennis courts, bicycles provided. No TV in rooms. 32 rooms. Major credit cards.

Bitter End Yacht Club $$$ *P.O. Box 46, Virgin Gorda, BVI; tel: 494-2745, 800-872-2392 (toll-free in the US); fax: 494-4756; www.beyc.com.* Located at the head of North Sound, with panoramic views. Extensive marina and harbor visited by cruise ships. Rooms furnished in batik and natural materials. All watersports included in the room charge. Restaurant, bar, pool, shops, children's club; in-room TV and VCR available on request. 90 rooms. Major credit cards.

Leverick Bay Hotel and Marina $$ *P.O. Box 63, The Valley, Virgin Gorda, BVI; tel: 495-7421, 800-848-7081 (toll-free in the US); fax: 495-7367; www.virgingordabvi.com.* Clinging to a hillside overlooking a well-equipped marina complex. Small beach, pool, spa, laundry, grocery store, gift shop. Some rooms with kitchens. 14 rooms. Major credit cards.

Little Dix Bay Resort $$$$ *P.O. Box 70, Virgin Gorda, BVI; tel: 495-5555, 800-928-3000 (toll-free in the US); fax: 495-5661; www.rosewood-hotels.com.* Near Spanish Town and the Virgin Gorda Yacht Club, set in magnificent grounds, this site has been on the list of outstanding resorts of the Caribbean for over 30 years. Three restaurants, two bars, seven tennis courts, palm-fringed beach. 102 rooms. Major credit cards.

Mango Bay Resort $$-$$$ *Mahoe Bay, P.O. Box 1062, Virgin Gorda, BVI; tel: 495-5672; fax: 495-5674; www.mangob-ayresort.com.* Overlooking Drake's Channel, ten minutes by car from Spanish Town. Set in landscaped tropical gardens. Cottages (with interior or outdoor kitchens) are on or near the reef-protected beach. 5 units. Major credit cards.

Olde Yard Inn $$-$$$ *P.O. Box 26, The Valley, Virgin Gorda, BVI; tel: 495-5544; 800-653-9273 (toll-free in the US); fax: 495-5986; www.travelxn.com/oldeyard.* With its peaceful, tropical-garden setting in the interior of the island, this hotel specializes in quiet seclusion. There is a celebrated library in two wooden pavilions with porches, including books, games, films, and a piano. Pool, Jacuzzi, open-air health club, restaurants. 14 rooms. Major credit cards.

Recommended Restaurants

Eating in the Virgin Islands means choosing from among a great variety of establishments serving local and international cuisine. Most of the larger resort hotels on the main islands have acclaimed dining rooms that are open to the public. There are also many independent establishments with a high reputation and a faithful clientele.

In the high season it would be sensible to make a reservation at any time. Out-of-season reservations should definitely be made on weekends. If you are a family, be sure to reserve in advance if you want to seat a large group at a definite time.

The following price categories are based on a three-course dinner, per person, without drinks. Prices are in US dollars and, generally, tend to be higher than average prices on the US mainland. Many restaurants will automatically add a gratuity or service charge to the bill; this will be indicated on the menu.

$$$$$	above $100
$$$$	$60–$100
$$$	$40–$60
$$	$25–$40
$	below $25

UNITED STATES VIRGIN ISLANDS

Note that all seven-digit local telephone numbers must be preceded by the **340** access code for the USVI when dialing from abroad.

St. Thomas

Banana Tree Grill $$$$ *Bluebeard's Castle, Charlotte Amalie; tel: 776-4050; e-mail: bananatree@islands.vi.* Formerly the "Entre Nous" restaurant, in a magnificent setting overlooking the harbor. Informal dining (Italian, Asian, Caribbean) with tropical décor. Open for dinner only Wed–Mon 6pm–9.30pm; reservations recommended. Major credit cards.

Café Wahoo $$$ *Piccola Marina, Red Hook; tel: 775-6350.* Dockside and open-air dining with European/Caribbean cuisine. Lunchtime sushi/tempura bar. Open Mon–Sat 11:30am–3pm for lunch, and daily 6pm–10pm for dinner; reservations recommended for dinner. Major credit cards.

Duffy's Love Shack $-$$ *Red Hook Plaza, Red Hook; tel: 779-2080; www.duffysloveshack.com.* Funky restaurant and bar located in the parking lot across from the main marina. American and Caribbean favorites are on the menu; the bar specializes in unusual cocktails. The place to be on a Saturday night. Open Sun–Thur 11am–1am, Fri–Sat 11am–2am. Major credit cards.

Eunice's Terrace $$-$$$ *Route 38, Smith Bay Road (near the Renaissance Grand); tel: 775-3975.* With what is said to be the best West Indian cuisine on St. Thomas, this restaurant has tropical décor. President and Mrs. Clinton had dinner here during a family holiday. Open daily for lunch 9am–4pm and dinner 5pm–11pm. Major credit cards.

Green House Bar and Restaurant $$-$$$ *Waterfront Highway, Storetvaer Gade, Charlotte Amalie; tel: 774-7998.* Partially open-air, informal restaurant with a sports-bar feel, in the center of Charlotte Amalie. American/Caribbean food. Live music late into the evening. Open 10:30am–1am daily; the bar closes when the last customer leaves. Major credit cards.

Hotel 1829 $$$ *Government Hill, Charlotte Amalie; tel: 776-1829, 800-524-2002 (toll-free in the US); fax: 776-4313.* Elegant restaurant in a historic house (now a hotel) above Charlotte Amalie. Extensive continental/Caribbean menu; soufflés a specialty. Open Mon–Sat 6pm–9pm for dinner only; reservations essential. Major credit cards.

St. John

Le Chateau de Bordeaux $$$$ *Centerline Road, Bordeaux Mountain; tel: 776-6611.* Perched on the highest lookout point on the island, with great views over Coral Bay and the BVI, this restaurant offers fine international cuisine and an extensive wine list. Open daily 6:30pm–10pm for dinner only; reservations recommended. Major credit cards.

Ellington's $$$$ *at Gallows Point Resort, Cruz Bay; tel: 693-8490.* Casual fine continental dining with a Caribbean flair; good wine cellar. Wonderful place to view the sunset over Pillsbury Sound. Open daily for lunch and dinner only. Major credit cards.

Fish Trap $$-$$$ *Raintree Shopping Center, Cruz Bay; tel: 693-9994; www.stjohnusvi.com/fishtrap.* Casual outdoor restaurant on a wooden deck, offering fresh fish specialties with an international flair; chicken and beef dishes as well. Open Tue–Sun 4:30pm–9:30pm for dinner only. Major credit cards.

Lime Inn $$-$$$ *Cruz Bay; tel: 776-6425 or 779-4199.* Colorful tropical courtyard setting in the heart of town. Extensive menu features international and Caribbean dishes; the lobster is justly famous. Open for lunch Mon–Fri 11:30am–3pm; for dinner Mon–Sat 5:30pm–10pm. Major credit cards.

Luscious Licks $-$$ *adjacent to Mongoose Junction, Cruz Bay; tel: 693-8400.* Health food café and specialty coffee house with an informal atmosphere, featuring juices, wheat-grass, and salads. Open Mon–Sat 10am–4pm. Cash only.

Stone Terrace $$$$ *Cruz Bay; tel: 693-9370; fax 693-8590; e-mail: raintree@islands.vi.* Elegant dining on an elevated terrace with a waterfront location overlooking Cruz Bay harbor. French, continental, and Caribbean selections accompanied by fine wines. Open daily 6:30pm–9:30pm for dinner only; reservations recommended. Major credit cards.

St. Croix

Blue Moon $$$-$$$$ *17 Strand St., Frederiksted; tel: 772-2222.* Atmospheric historic building on the waterfront with a mixture of New Orleans creole, French bistro, and vegetarian dishes. Live jazz weekends. Open for lunch Tue–Fri 11:30am–2pm, for dinner Tue–Sun 6pm–10:30pm, for Sunday brunch 11am–2pm; reservations recommended. Major credit cards.

The Galleon $$$-$$$$ *on Route 82 (East End Road) at Green Cay Marina, Teague Bay; tel: 773-9949.* Fine waterfront dining with an extensive French and northern Italian menu; popular with locals and visitors. Open daily 7pm–11pm for dinner only. Major credit cards.

Indies $$$ *55–56 Company St., Christiansted; tel: 692-9440.* Set in an 18th-century courtyard with abundant tropical plants, Indies offers Caribbean-style cuisine with an emphasis on fresh fish dishes. Live music Thursday and Saturday nights, when it gets extremely busy. The place to meet young, professional Cruzans. Open for lunch Mon–Fri 11:30am–2:30pm, for dinner daily 6pm–10:30pm; reservations recommended. Major credit cards.

Tivoli Gardens $$$ *upstairs in the Pan Am Pavilion, Queen Cross and Strand streets, Christiansted; tel: 773-6782.* Alfresco dining in the heart of Christiansted. The restaurant has a garden atmosphere with plants and a collection of European sculptures. Continental menu, but famed for lobster dishes. Live guitar music in the evenings. Open for lunch Mon–Fri 11:15am–2:30pm, for dinner daily 6pm–9:30pm. Major credit cards.

Top Hat $$$$-$$$$$ *52 Company St. (at Market Square), Christiansted; tel: 773-2346.* In a beautifully restored townhouse full of Scandinavian charm, the Danish owners have created a well-regarded menu of local seafood along with Continental (including Scandinavian) dishes. The cozy bar is full of pictures of famous clients. Open daily 6:30pm–10pm (closed May–August); reservations recommended. Major credit cards.

BRITISH VIRGIN ISLANDS

Note that all seven-digit local phone numbers must be preceded by the **284** access code for the BVI when dialing from abroad.

Tortola

Fish Trap $$-$$$ *Columbus Centre, Road Town; tel: 494-3626.* An open-air seafood restaurant serving international cuisine including lobster, conch fritters, chicken teriyaki, and some Mexican dishes. Open for lunch Mon–Sat 11:30am–3pm, for dinner daily 6:30pm–11pm. Major credit cards.

Last Resort Island Restaurant $$$-$$$$ *Trellis Bay, Beef Island; tel: 495-2520; VHF Channel 16.* Situated on a small island in Trellis Bay and accessible only by a boat or ferry that you call by phone from shore. Dinner buffet includes fish and roast beef. Open daily for lunch 12:30pm–2pm and for dinner at 7pm (with cabaret at 9pm). Major credit cards.

Mrs. Scatcliffe's Bar and Restaurant $$-$$$ *Carrot Bay (across from primary school); tel: 495-4556.* The place to get local food, with home-grown vegetables and fruits served at Mrs. Scatcliffe's house. Open for lunch Mon–Fri noon–2pm, and for dinner daily 7pm–8:30pm; make reservations by 5:30pm. Cash only.

Pusser's Landing $$-$$$ *Soper's Hole, Frenchman's Cay; tel: 495-4554.* International cuisine (snacks, chicken wings, and pizza) along with pasta, chicken, and meat entrées. Open daily for lunch 11am–3pm and for dinner 6pm–10pm. Major credit cards.

Skyworld $$$-$$$$ *located off Joe's Hill Road above Road Town; tel: 494-3567; fax: 495-9546.* Offers panoramic views of Tortola and surrounding islands—an ideal place to escape the heat of the day. Imaginative international and Caribbean menu. Open daily for lunch 11:30am–2:30pm and dinner (by reservation) 5pm–7:45pm. Major credit cards.

Virgin Gorda

Biras Creek Resort $$$$ *North Sound, near Bitter End; tel: 494-3555; fax: 494-3553.* Award-winning international cuisine in this elegant tower-top restaurant overlooking North Sound.

The emphasis is on fresh fish and produce. Five-course fixed-price dinner menu. Open daily for breakfast 8am–10am, for lunch 1pm–2pm, and for dinner 7pm–9pm; reservations essential for dinner; dress code for dinner. Major credit cards.

Little Dix Bay Resort $$$$ *near Spanish Town and Virgin Gorda Yacht Club; tel: 495-5555, ext. 174.* Spacious open-air dining on the terrace with an Indonesian-style roof. Sophisticated international menu that changes daily; buffet lunch is particularly good. Open daily for lunch 12:30pm–2pm and dinner 7pm–9pm; reservations recommended. Major credit cards.

Olde Yard Inn $$$-$$$$ *the Valley; tel: 495-5544, 800-653-9273 (toll-free in the US); fax: 495-5986.* Charming restaurant in a quiet, secluded hotel, featuring homemade soups and local seafood. Classical music plays in the background. Open daily for lunch 11am–2pm and dinner 6pm–9:30pm. Major credit cards.

Top of the Baths $$$ *at entrance to the Baths, the Valley; tel: 495-5497; VHF Channel 16.* Located at the top of the hill above the Baths (with great views of Drake's Passage and the BVI), this restaurant has an international menu with indoor and outdoor dining along with a small swimming pool where you can cool off. Open daily for breakfast 8am–10:30am, lunch 11am–6pm, and dinner 6pm–10pm. Major credit cards.

Jost Van Dyke

Foxy's $$-$$$ *at Great Harbour; tel: 495-9258; VHF Channel 16.* Informal beach bar/restaurant (shoes are optional) with barbecue dishes, fresh fish, and "roadies" (large stuffed tortillas). Foxy will serenade you with his unique calypso songs. Open daily for lunch from noon–2:30pm, for dinner 6:30pm–9pm; barbecue buffet Fri–Sat 7:30pm–9pm; dinner reservations required by 5pm daily. Major credit cards.

INDEX

Berlitz Puts The World In Your Pocket

Berlitz speaks the language of travel. Its Pocket Guides take you to more than 110 destinations and its phrase books, pocket dictionaries, and cassette and CD language packs help you communicate when you get there.